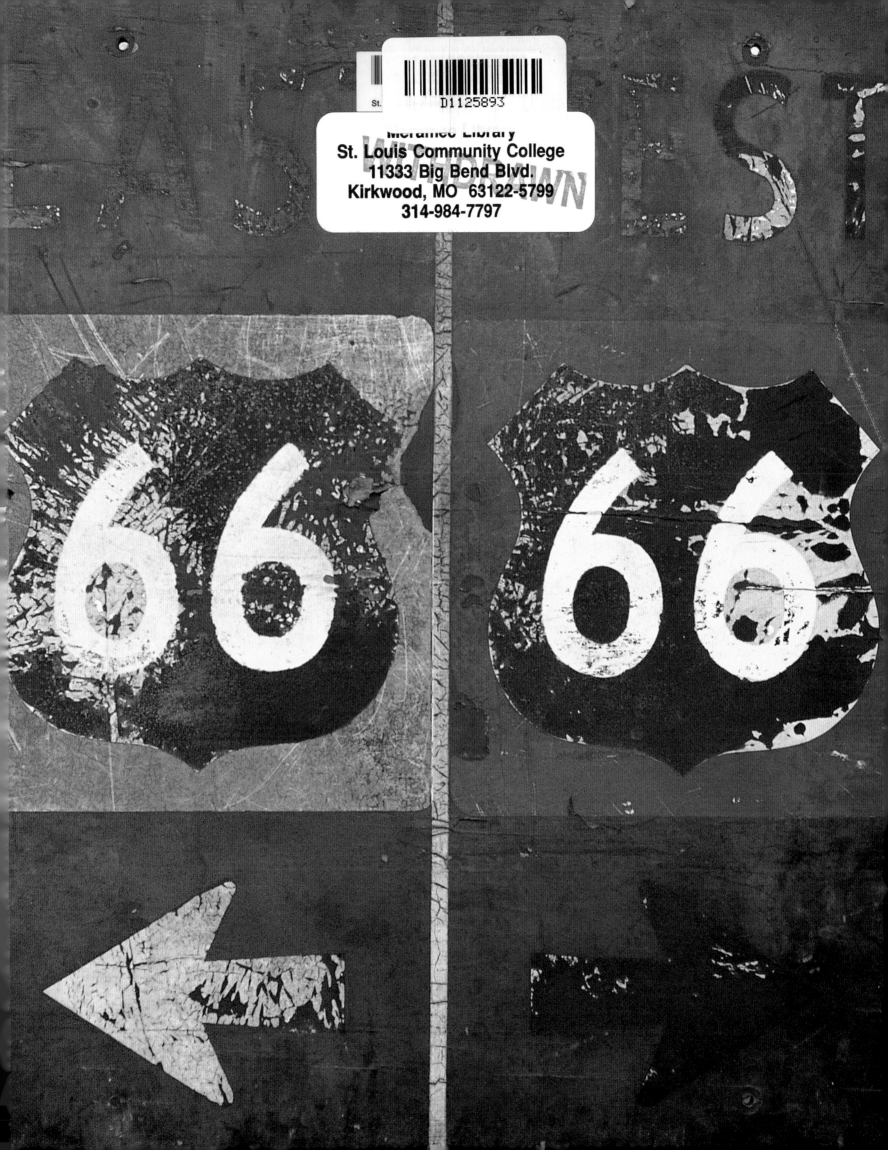

Meramec Library
St. Louis Community College
11333 Big Bend Blvd.
Kirkwood, MO 63122-5799
314-984-7797

D1125893

WITHDRAWN

St. Louis Community College
at Meramec
Library

5/01

ROADSIDE

AMERICA

THE AUTOMOBILE AND THE AMERICAN DREAM

STEAK n SHAKE
TRU-FLAVOR SHAKES
GRINDING ONLY GOV'T
22-313
24-947

ROADSIDE AMERICA

THE AUTOMOBILE AND THE AMERICAN DREAM

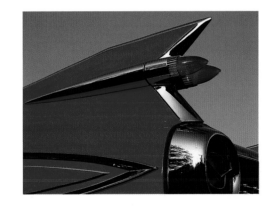

BY LUCINDA LEWIS

HARRY N. ABRAMS, INC., PUBLISHERS

CONTENTS

1933 Pierce Arrow Silver Arrow Rear detail

ACKNOWLEDGMENTS

The only way a project like this can succeed is through the shared enthusiasm and cooperation of the many car and location owners featured in this book. I would like to cite the many car clubs, in particular the Classic Car Club of America and the Antique Automobile Club of America, who assisted me in locating special cars in remote parts of America. The reader will notice that most of the photographs were made before dawn or just after dusk. This requirement wrested many bleary-eyed car owners from their beds and required business owners and managers to make special arrangements for us to have parking access and neon lights glowing at times when they would not normally be available. For all of those who lost hours of sleep, I am grateful. You have helped record a bit of America history on film.

I am especially appreciative to Jeffrey Sturges for helping immeasurably with the writing of this book. His mastery of the English language and rapier wit helped my arcane knowledge of automobiles and roadside America come alive. To my editor, Ruth Peltason, who somehow made everything better. And to Dana Sloan for her book design wizardry, and to my agent Danny Simon for believing in the project.

On the photography front, I tip my hat to Volker Dencks for his visual acumen, production skills, and ability to drive our overloaded minivan many hours on too little sleep. And to Janet Burt and her assistant, Valerie Farias, whose patience and organizational skills kept the office humming. Thanks to Mike Lee at Digital Color Lab and Florence Tsang for her digital mastery. Michel Karman of A & I exhibitions did an extraordinary job printing the black-and-white images reproduced in the book.

I wish to thank the many car culture fans across America who have taken the time to write and phone me with recommendations for the cars and locations featured in this book. Your support helps sustain me whenever I stop to wonder why in the world I am doing this. Many thanks are also due to the readers of *Modern Maturity* magazine who took the time to write me letters describing their car journeys across Route 66 in days gone past.

This book is dedicated to my dad for turning me onto wings and wheels, and to my mother for giving me the life skills to harness my over-active imagination to reality. And last but not least, to my husband, John, for his creativity, endless patience, and willingness to sit white-knuckled beside me while I try to see how fast the latest sports car will go.

Happy Motoring in the 21st Century!

INTRODUCTION

When people discover I'm a photographer, they usually assume I shoot fashion. "No," I say, "I shoot cars." At that point my listener generally comes back with either "That's nice, dearie" or silence, followed by the hesitant question, "Cars?" From here the conversation can veer off in different directions, but we almost always return to the cars this person has owned and cherished or the cars they have lusted after. Americans frequently measure their lives in terms of the cars they've owned. Births, deaths, graduations, marriages, and other milestones are often remembered by the cars that ferried participants to and from an event. Once we finish discussing such past cars, the inevitable question arises, "Why is a nice girl like you photographing cars?"

There's no easy answer, but for me a prime attraction of cars has always been freedom of movement. If you've got wheels, you've got a ticket to ride. I've always been highly mobile and attracted to anything that could take me faster and farther. My mother began running after me when I stood up and began to walk at seven months. At four years old I learned to drive: my Dad and I had a deal where he pushed the pedals and I steered the car from his lap.

As I grew older, the real thrill lay in venturing out of our yard by myself. Like most kids, I had a bicycle and can tell you that nothing pleased me more than sailing out into the vast unknown, pumping the pedals as hard as I could. With the wind whipping through my pony tail and the flapping syncopation of the playing cards I had clothes-pinned to my back wheel spokes, I was king of the world. My electric blue '62 Schwinn and I would zip around my "racetrack" (the single suburban block I was permitted to circumnavigate) over and over until my mother sent one of my little sisters to flag me in.

Car trips were the greatest thrill of all. Mom would load all three girls into our 1963 Buick Skylark for the weekly jaunt to visit our grandparents. Naturally we fought over the right to sit in the front seat, so we could gloat about its commanding view of the road to the sisters stuck in the back. The sisters had one ironclad pact, however. When the front-seat spotter spied a roadside treat—such as Dairy Queen—her responsibility was to launch the campaign for Mom to pull over. Quickly the monotonous chant would rise—"Dairy Queen, Dairy Queen, Dairy Queen"—,our voices united in a fervent plea that became more and more desperate as we neared the coveted treat.

Our goal? The universal goal of pleading children—to play on Mom's heartstrings, trying to convince her we might keel over without a chocolate-dipped DQ twirl cone. Sometimes Mom stopped and sometimes she didn't. When she did, we often tortured ourselves with contests to see who could drink their icy cold Mr. Misty fastest. The winner received the honor of a splitting headache. When

chronically short-handed editor appointed me darkroom assistant. Under the red glow of a Kodak safelight, and over the driving beat of Iron Butterfly, he shouted obtuse directions on how to gently rock the developing trays to reveal the latent photograph. I was transfixed as an image floated to life against the milky-white paper. To this day, that magic has never left me. I learned to see through the camera. Whether or not I picked up a camera to earn my living, the world would never be the same.

My first paying job in photography was printing portraits for a local baby photographer. This gentleman taught me how to bestow a beatific glow to each and every child's chubby face by printing the image through an old nylon stocking. By my college graduation I knew for certain I did not want to be a baby photographer. Nonetheless, flying and photography chased any thoughts of law school right out the window. Photography mingled naturally with flying: I had always loved the way the earth formed intricate patterns as it flowed beneath the wings of my airplane. As I developed my photography skills, I realized I could commingle flying and photography to record these passing abstractions from the plane.

My first business was taking aerial photographs of the Research Triangle Park, a pioneering North Carolina think tank. Each month, I would document the construction of this massive corporate headquarters. Gently banking my rented plane, I would simply open the window and lean out to snap the photos. After days in my darkroom, I'd zip down the highway in my Datsun 280Z and sell my photos to the construction companies. It didn't take me long to figure out that the aesthetic satisfactions of aerial photography were as limited as the paychecks. My father agreed, declaring "You're no ordinary dummy," and so the non-ordinary dummy packed up and moved to San Francisco in search of more compelling images.

While living in San Francisco, I continued to fly, primarily out of Gnoss Field in Marin County. On one of my weekend jaunts I met another aerial photographer who had an assignment to photograph automobiles for a book called *American Cars,* to be authored by Leon Mandel. I agreed to spend a couple of weeks helping set up a studio at the Harrah's Automobile Collection in Reno, Nevada. At that time, Harrah's was the world's largest car collection. Boasting some fourteen hundred automobiles, the museum was a mecca for car enthusiasts around the world. I thought I knew something about cars until I reached Harrah's.

When I walked into Harrah's lavish showroom I was stupefied to discover cars I'd never even heard of, such as the Moon Mobile, the Dymaxion, the 1912 Baker Electric car, and more. The sculptural heft of these rolling wonders blew my mind. Harrah's marked a turning point for me. My prophetic moment came while making the photograph of the 1929 Duesenberg found on page 57. Lying flat on my back underneath the car, I was struggling to capture its chrome-laden grill against the puffy white clouds floating above. Literally and figuratively, that Duesenberg was about to run over me. As the shutter clicked I knew I had met my destiny. I was hooked.

My taste of Harrah's turned me into a classic car junkie, searching out four-wheeled thoroughbreds wherever I could find them. With camera in hand, I attended every Concours d'Elégance car show in Northern California, enjoying the crème de la crème of the automotive set. I loved the way rich and poor are united by the dream these automobiles represent. Visiting a car show, a car maven of modest means can chat with the wealthy owner of a much-coveted car whom he might never otherwise meet. Their joint enthusiasm creates a common bond, bridging an economic gap which can separate people in ordinary life. More than a mere transportation device full of oil and gasoline, a car is a vessel sheltering hopes and dreams.

After realizing I was born to shoot cars, the next step was figuring out how to educate myself in this relatively arcane field. There's no specific curriculum for a car photographer, no college to attend. I knew what I responded to in the cars—their sumptuous shapes and the wonderful way light spilled across their sheet metal. Very quickly I discovered these attributes were not always of interest to a true or "purist" car enthusiast. My newfound car buddies would make comments about my work like, "Nice photo, but you've got it all wrong—the news in this car is that it's supercharged and you can't even see that from this angle."

Properly chastised, I set out to learn as much as possible about cars before I picked up the camera again. The irreverent university I attended for this degree of higher education was known as the Candy Store. Currently housed in an elegant old Packard showroom in the heart of Burlingame, California (just south of San Francisco), the Candy Store occupied more humble surroundings when I first became acquainted with it. The original Candy Store was an old warehouse in a questionable part of town. It is and always has been a clubhouse of sorts, a place for car buffs to congregate and display some of their great classic cars.

Friday afternoons at the Candy Store, Frenchy (Jacques Harguindegay), Russell Head, Don Klusmann, J. Heumann, or whoever happened to be lazily polishing chrome or changing oil would hold forth over a bottle of wine. I tried never to miss it. We would set up a row of chairs like theater seats in front of the scintillating cast of cars crammed in the warehouse. After a pop of the cork, the gurus would begin the evening's discourse. These guys were world-class experts on their subject. My sole credential was an enthusiasm for their cars that nearly matched their own.

With the experts' help I began photographing their fantastic automobiles. I scoured the Bay Area for the location that best reflected the personality of an automotive subject and together we'd motor off to make the portrait. While I was shooting they would lecture me on the unique aspects of their car, pointing out a seductive belt line or the compound curves of a particularly intricate fender. In between shoots I studied books borrowed from their automotive libraries. Over time I assembled a portfolio of automotive photography that I circulated among the automotive magazines. The portfolio was spectacular in one regard only—the custom coachbuilt cars owned by my pals at the Candy Store.

My plan worked. The first editor to cross the gender barrier by giving me an automotive photography assignment was Leon Mandel at *Autoweek*. Leon and I had been friends since my work at Harrah's on his book. He was my first instructor: I can only thank the Lord that Leon had a daughter whom he and his lovely wife, Olivia, had raised with the same freewheeling attitude my parents had toward me. Taking pity on my struggle for work, Leon gave me my first byline at the weekly.

Slowly I began getting editorial assignments from other car magazines. This was no easy feat in the early 1980s, when women photographing cars were scarce as hen's teeth (to my knowledge there was only one other woman shooting cars at the time). My crash course at the Candy Store gave me the expertise necessary to win over reluctant magazine editors. The fact that I knew more about some of these one-of-a-kind classics than the editors themselves (until they'd done their research) enabled me to convince them I could handle the job. Once I'd earned my wings shooting vintage sheet metal for the magazines, I began receiving new car assignments.

After struggling to learn photography and the world of automobiles that would be my subject, I faced a new challenge—learning to produce advertising-quality photographs. Vintage car portraits are one thing, but advertising is tough! Early on in this process, for example, it struck me how difficult it was to keep stray light reflections off the sides of cars. These rogue reflections distract horribly from seeing the true lines of the vehicles and are devilishly hard to avoid. It took a professional car photographer, Rob Gage, to teach me the subtleties of lighting.

A well-known advertising photographer, Rob occasionally gave workshops for other photographers. I was still hanging out with the Candy Store gurus when the opportunity to take a seminar from Rob came up. I jumped on it and Rob and I became good friends, despite the constant barrage of lighting questions I put to him. Again, another saint to the rescue. Rob sent me out on the road to scout locations for him and then analyzed every location in terms of its advantages and disadvantages, the best time of day to photograph there, and other potential problems. What a gift.

Finally, I produced a portfolio even I was comfortable with and set out for the Motor City in search of big game—the advertising assignment. I hit the pavement armed with a list of fifteen or so art directors to see in four days. My first appointment was with the head art director of one of Detroit's "Big Three" truck divisions. I showed up straight from the airport and he began to review my book. Every few moments he'd murmur appreciatively and say something like, "nice, very nice." I was beginning to envision those big bucks rolling in. As he flipped through my transparencies he asked, "Now who is it you represent? He's very good."

"Myself," I replied quietly. "Very nice," he'd say, "What did you say his name was?" "It's me," I said. "I'm the photographer." "Oh," then he paused to look at me and announced, "I have girls," as he pointed proudly to photos of his daughters propped on his desk. I stared at him, dumbfounded. "Then you should help me," I blurted. Now it was his turn to stare. At length he picked up the phone and dialed a friend in the business. "Joe," he said, "I've got someone you just have to meet. When can you see her?" He closed the conversation with, "You owe me one, buddy—she's a real looker." Leaving the meeting in a daze, I drove straight to the 7-Eleven and bought a six-pack of beer and a pound-bag of peanut M&Ms. I sat in the parking lot and polished them both off. It was going to be a long week in Detroit.

As I moved into the big league of automotive advertising, my love of cars sustained me through the beer-and-M&Ms days found in anyone's career. Several art directors tried to focus me on shooting studio setups. While I relish the purity of studio photography, my first love has continued to be the challenge of shooting on location.

On location shoots, I usually expose film in the brief time (about fifteen minutes) just before the sun rises or immediately after it sets. During these precious minutes the entire heavenly dome of sky becomes one gigantic light source, radiating a glow that rolls like warm caramel across a car's sheet metal. These interludes—known for good reason as Magic Hour—are times of fierce concentration for me: hopefully, they're the time I am able to make all the preparation pay off.

The days and hours prior to these minutes are full of urgency as we prepare. Deploying a fleet of assistants, I scout the location, position the car, and detail it in preparation for the shot. Selecting the right lens is pivotal, as is setting lights, generator, and reflectors. These elements and more must be in place before I can even begin to expose film. The moment the light is right, it's a race against the clock as my heightened reactions try to shape the elements into a final impression.

At times making a photo becomes a contest of wills. Many of the photographs in this book haunted my ambitious imagination long before car met film. When the time comes to make my vision a reality, I am faced with odds that sometimes seem insurmountable. The pivotal instance where reality seemed to have a contract out on my ambition was the portrait I made of the two-tone 1933 Duesenberg found on page 47.

This photograph is unique because there was no location. For insurance reasons, the Duesenberg had to stay on the premises of Harrah's, forcing me to build a set around the car. Harrah's was delighted when I first told them I had an idea how to photograph the Dusie in their parking lot. "Come on up," they said, "the weather's great." I loaded my car with boxes of cheap black-and-white linoleum tiles, rallied my assistants in Reno (including several off-duty F14 pilots), and headed for Harrah's. Surely this would be a piece of cake.

On a beautiful October day in the Harrah's parking lot we built a fifty-foot-black wall to control the light, anchored it, and rolled out the seductive Duesenberg. Positioning myself and the camera atop a hydraulic airplane lift from the local airport, I began to compose the shot by striking a chalk line at the base of my camera's field of view and laying out the black-and-white tiles. Just after midday, I noticed the tiles were beginning to veer off to the left. It would be too late to correct the error and make the shot before sundown. Oh well. We meticulously packed everything up, vowing to be more careful tomorrow.

As we laid out the tiles the next day, the temperature began to drop. In Reno. In the morning. By midday the tiles were so cold they were snapping apart before we could get them on the ground. Worse yet, I could see that despite our efforts the columns of tiles were again veering off to the left! Staring down at my "great idea" from my hydraulic perch I felt ready to slit my throat. Ellis, one of the auto mechanics from the museum, climbed up to see what the problem was. Taking one look, he spat out "Car's not square." "What?" I asked in disbelief.

Ellis explained that in the pre-computer era of 1933, one-of-a-kind cars like the Duesenberg were built using a technique from boat construction called lofting. One guy would climb into the workshop rafters holding a knotted cord: the workers below would use the cord to spot where the swell of the fenders and grill should end. This marking would determine the wooden frame across which the metal skin of the car would be beaten into shape. Like a handmade boat, the Duesenberg was built by approximation rather than by measurement. I was trying to lay a grid around a car that was not square: every error would be magnified!

This is the point where logic told me to go home. Instead, I stayed up all night listening to the chill wind whip through the trees—a wind that also blew down our wall. Fortunately for me, the never-say-die carpenter on my crew had heard the wind and showed up the next morning prepared to raise the Titanic. We put the wall back up and phoned a surveyor who helped me shoot sight lines to cheat the tiles. We constructed fake tiles of uneven dimensions to create the illusion of symmetry. With sunset fast approaching, we laid down the remaining fake tiles. It worked! The fake looked more real than the real! I nailed the shot. Or did the car nail me?

The checkered Dusie taught me that grand ideas don't necessarily make for the greatest pictures. Despite my pride at having pulled off the logistical challenge of the shoot, I have since realized that the cerebral qualities of this image are less than fulfilling for me. The texture of real life beckoned: the real world of the American roadside was my inspiration. Cars are most themselves in their natural habitat. They belong on the road. And they belong to the road.

It didn't take long for me to realize that great locations were harder to find than great cars. Cars can be protected in garages by owners who gentle them like babies. Locations, on the other hand, are subject to the vagaries of weather and the inevitable effects of progress. In turning to location photography, I started with the roadside attractions I remembered from my youth. So many had disappeared; moreover, the people and habits that created them had disappeared as well. Where did they all go?

Attempting to answer this question, I became more and more fascinated with the impact that generations of automobiles have had upon the landscape of our lives. Location work allowed for a level of interpretation and social comment that I had never thought to reach for in my advertising photography. The focus of my work shifted as I set about trying to record our car culture. In the process I created a portrait of roadside America.

My search for locations took me across an America not shown in glossy travel brochures—the "two-lane" America I discovered and fell in love with on my cross-country tour so long ago. Shaped by the automobile of the common man, this America features vast lonely vistas punctuated by neon outposts that signal the presence of life on the edge of nowhere. On these roads—Route 66 most prominently—Giant Donuts and outlandish Milk Bottles vie for the passing motorist's attention alongside stainless steel-clad diners gleaming like craft from another world.

These roadside attractions amalgamate fierce individuality, practicality, and sheer wackiness in a way that uniquely embodies the American frontier spirit. Realizing that these oddities were disappearing as America ceases to be a frontier, I resolved to commemorate as many of them as I could. Hence was born, many years and thousands of miles ago, the "Roadside America" technique and photographic style that have generated this book.

By now I have developed something of a modus operandi in my approach. Once I identify a location that catches my fancy, I try to find the car or cars that define the essential feeling of the place. Many of these photos haunt me, in one form or another, long before I commit them to film. I owe a tremendous debt to the movies: many of my photographs are scene creations influenced by my love of cinema. My goal is always to make tangible the memories that lie dormant in these roadside attractions—to peel away the layers of time and put the viewer in an imaginative driver's seat, envisioning what it might have been like to drive into this particular location during its heyday in a car of the period.

Route 66 has been a central avenue of my pilgrimage because that's where most vintage roadside America icons still survive. In a curious way, the federal decision in the 1950s to decommission Route 66 and bypass it with the interstate highway system saved some American cultural history by cutting off Route 66 locations from the effects of traffic and time. The reduced traffic along the old road reduced budgets for "modernization," thereby leaving many of its vintage locations relatively intact.

Despite being wiped off our highway maps, the Main Street of America lived on in the collective memories of the old-timers who had traveled it and/or had grown up along it. The old Route 66 has blossomed with new life since the late 1970s, as nostalgic travelers began retracing the path so many had taken along the Mother Road. These travelers proved eager patrons of the famed roadside establishments that had not fallen prey to corporate franchises. I have tried to include as many of these worthy survivors as possible in my documentation of an America seen from the roadside.

As we all know, Route 66 is no longer an easy road to travel. I could never have achieved the documentation I have without help from many people, prominent among them producer Volker Dencks. Years ago, while working on *Porsche: The Fine Art of the Sports Car*, I faxed a contact in Germany seeking an assistant for a shooting assignment at the Porsche Museum. Volker faxed me back and fate must have a hand in it: we got along like a Ferrari in high gear and have continued to work together across the years and continents.

With Volker I have driven almost ninety-five hundred miles photographing Route 66, crisscrossing the remaining two-lane highway in a Dodge minivan chock-a-block with generator, lights, cameras, and assorted road accoutrements. Come to think of it, our overloaded minivan doesn't look too different from those famous WPA–era photographs of the listing Model T Fords that ferried entire families westward with their iron skillets and chairs lashed to the roofs.

We started out in search of the remaining Route 66 roadside attractions: in the end we found much more. It's a big country out there, folks, lest we forget it. Our repeated journeys between Los Angeles and Chicago have exposed us to myriad cultures, regional foods, and distinctive personalities that serve to remind us that the American experience is as varied as the country is huge. Route 66 was just the start as we branched out in search of even less-known roadside attractions of the regional highways.

Finding distinctive automobiles in remote corners of America is always difficult and sometimes downright impossible. Our roadside routine usually has us spending the "bad light hours" (midday) tracking down cars. On a road trip we generally try to line up cars two or three days in advance of arriving at a particular location. The scouting is usually accomplished via telephone.

The routine goes something like this: "Hello, my name is Cindy/Walter (Volker has given up trying to use his real name outside of big cities). I'm doing a photography project on Roadside America. Joe Blow gave me your name and said you had a 1941 Chevy convertible. Pause. Well, we'd like to take a photograph of your car in front of a scenic Route 66 landmark. Oh, you hurt your back. That's too bad. And your mother died—gee. I'm really sorry. No, I don't know where that is. The funeral's tomorrow? You're going to carry her casket in the Chevy—oh I see, Well, yes, it is a shock, isn't it? Do you know any one else who might have a car? Jerry Smith? Great. Do you happen to have his phone number? Uh huh—he's married to Doris from White Oak—yes, do you think it's in the phone book under Doris or Jerry? Oh, he just got out of jail—that's good. You think it's under Doris. O.K." And so it goes. Phone call after phone call. Why do I do it?

I'd be lying if I didn't confess to loving it. There are mornings that I question my sanity—when I wake up to shoot at 3:30 A.M. with an Excedrin PM hangover (sometimes I get so wound up it's hard to sleep) and find myself sitting in a 60s coffee shop extravaganza being attended by an 8-months-and-counting pregnant waitress who is so friendly it makes my teeth hurt. But the satisfaction when the shutter clicks on an image I dreamed of the night before more than compensates for passing annoyances of the road. The knowledge that our roadside heritage is fast fading from the landscape is also a factor that drives me.

My self-appointed mission is to record our twentieth-century car culture on film and I can tell you it's a race against the wrecking ball. Many of the locations in this book have been destroyed since the photos were made. The dominance of corporate franchises and our peculiarly American compulsion to constantly reinvent ourselves result in a daily transformation of the landscape. The rise of the automobile spawned the glorious tourist traps, neon-drenched diners, drive-in movie theaters, and last-chance gas stations that pepper our landscape. My job is to bring that roadside back to life by reuniting it with some of the fabulous automobiles that streaked across it in its heyday.

As a photographer, I am happy to have captured some of our American roadside on film. Other cultures have managed to preserve bits and pieces of their heritage; in this country we have a penchant toward dismissing our history. If it's not branded as high art, we tend to discard it. Our American jazz, our folk art, movies, even our roadside icons are just now being understood as something to commemorate and celebrate. But what does that mean?

As we stand on the brink of a new millennium, there is reason for us to pause. Much as that 1929 Duesenberg was about to run over me, it seems the car has now run over America.

Cartoonist R. Crumb made an animated short film titled *A Brief History of America*. Picture this: first, there is the pristine American countryside with native animals grazing, then a dirt road through this landscape with carts and wagon trains crossing. Time passes and we see a Model T painfully motoring across the deeply rutted road. Then finally today, this same bit of landscape is an intersection paved in concrete with fourteen stoplights, road signs, gas stations, and pedestrian walk signals trying to orchestrate the flow of bumper-to-bumper traffic.

Orson Welles's film *The Magnificent Ambersons*—set at the turn of this century—features an argument about the rise of the automobile. Eugene Morgan, a fictional inventor of the automobile, muses aloud: "With all their speed forward they may be a step backwards in civilization. Maybe they won't add to the beauty of the world or the life of men's souls—I'm not sure. But automobiles have come and almost all outward things are going to be different because of what they bring. They're going to alter war and they're going to alter peace and I think men's minds are going to change in subtle ways because of automobiles."

Welles was right: the automobile has changed the way men think. But another world view holds that the automobile has brought freedom and opportunity to millions who otherwise would not have had it. Aren't automobiles one of the purest manifestations of our yearning to be free? Like my early adventures behind the wheel of my Schwinn bicycle, these images represent my interpretation of freedom in motion.

Besides, who can deny that glorious feeling when you're heading out into the great unknown with a full tank of gas?

1. REINVENTING THE BUGGY 1895-1915

AS THE NINETEENTH CENTURY METAMORPHOSED into the twentieth, America was a nation on the move. Americans were striving to be "thoroughly modern" and mobility was the centerpiece of the modern way. Migrating from foot to horse to steam train, Americans delighted in the freedom afforded by these increasingly quick forms of locomotion. The widespread introduction of the bicycle gave the individual a personal autonomy previously experienced only on horseback. With its tires and spokes, the bicycle helped spark a growing fascination with the automobile as it motored its way into our collective consciousness.

America, widely regarded as a nation of tinkers, turned its inventiveness to the automobile in the late 1890s. Many of our best inventors (soon to become early automotive industrialists) came from the bicycle trade or such industries as gun manufacturing, with exacting technical specifications. Early automotive designs featured varied sources of propulsion: steam, gasoline, and electricity all had their proponents.

With its round beveled windshield and snazzy brass trim, this 1910 Marion Special Roadster declares its complete independence from the horse-and-buggy era. This is a new style—a style shaped by speed.

Top: 1900 Packard
Runabout wheel
Bottom: 1909 Ford
Model T Touring dash

Although prospective drivers were not re-quired to pass skill tests, most states did issue driving licenses and required an owner to register his or her car. By 1900 there were eight thousand automobiles registered in the United States.

As a potential buyer at the time, you prob-ably read about the latest automotive devel-opments in the newspaper. In 1901, it would have been hard to miss the publicity surround-ing the new 1901 Curved Dash Oldsmobile as it journeyed from Detroit to the New York Auto Show. The 850-mile trip took seven days: blowouts in the Olds's balloon tires were the biggest obstacle. If you were impressed by this motoring achievement and comfortably well off, you may have been enticed to order a car from your nearest dealer. Unless you lived in a town with a dealership, your car arrived by rail. Most likely you learned to drive by reading the owner's manual for the make and model of the car that you bought.

Soon after their introduction, automobiles assumed a position they have held ever since—they conferred status. As toys for the rich they segregated those with and without money at a glance. Much of the early status of automobiles resulted from their scarcity: from 1903 to 1904, for example, there were only twenty-two Buicks built! Unless you were a doctor, your motivation for buying an auto-mobile was probably pure pleasure. But one soon discovered it was difficult and scary to drive the ill-smelling beasts. Worst of all, you had to don a new suit of clothes for the task: from the moment you took to the road, you were enveloped in a cloud of dust and/or oil beaten up from the macadam beneath. Hats, goggles, dusters, driving gloves, and lap robes were necessary armor to face the joys and perils of the early highway.

Road racing became increasingly popular and proved to be a great advertising device for the new automotive inventors. Henry Ford started out as one of the earliest road racers. The nascent auto-mobile industry began staging spectacular racing events to build publicity for its wares. In 1905, Oldsmobile sent two cars to the Lewis & Clark Exposition in Portland, Oregon. And three years later, the international New York-to-Paris race attracted phenomenal interest.

Henry Ford was eventually lured away from the racetrack and into production with a clear vision of the automobile he would build. "I will build a car for the great multitude. It will be large enough for the family, but small enough for the individual to run and care for. It will be constructed of the best materials, by the best men to be hired, after the simplest designs that modern engineering can devise. But it will be low in price so that no man making a good salary will be unable to own one— and enjoy with his family the blessings of hours of pleasure in God's great open spaces."

In 1908 the introduction of the Ford Model T realized Henry's dream at the astonishingly low price of $850. Ford introduced efficient assembly-line techniques and paid his workers well with the idea that they would become his best customers. He was right. As production grew, the price of the Model T fell to an astounding $250 by 1922 and Ford employees were major buyers.

With a reliable and affordable car available at last, the middle classes took to the automobile in droves. But the highways were far from a bed of roses. Many of the early cars boasted top speeds of 60 MPH: speeding became a growing problem as traffic enforcement lagged behind the growth of the

1903 Ford Rear Entrance Toneau detail

1911 Pope-Hartford badge

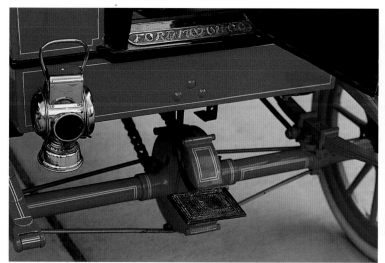

Above: Henry Ford built the "999" as an experimental racer in 1902. As one of America's earliest automotive tinkerers, Ford explored a number of engineering concepts on his own before forming the Ford Motor Car Company. Barney Oldfield, a famous race car driver of the era, drove this car to victory over the famous Winton Bullet in 1903. Later, with Henry Ford behind the wheel (or tiller, as it was then called), the car broke the land speed record at 91 MPH on Michigan's frozen Lake St. Clair.
Left: 1902 Ford "999" engine detail

Above: 1911 Crane Simplex 4-Passenger Tourabout detail

automotive culture. Most townships posted speed limits of 12 MPH, but few drivers obeyed this draconian code. Critics claimed that the automobile brought out the devil in people, pointing out that some speed-crazed individuals even took out second mortgages to buy a car.

Roadside businesses geared to the automobile were practically nonexistent in the beginning. The local general store was your source for gasoline (costing between 6 and 18 cents per gallon in 1902), tire patch kits, and spark plugs. More complex repairs required parts from your nearest dealer, which could be a significant distance. Fortunately, many livery stable operations sensed the future overtaking them and began to act as automotive agents while still caring for the horses that were the car's main competitor until the 1920s.

As the number of automobiles grew, curbside pumps became increasingly dangerous. Not only did the line of cars waiting by the pump cause the first traffic jams, the flammable gasoline located so close to speeding cars represented accidents just waiting to happen. In the northeast, oil companies gradually began to experiment with filling stations that would allow for a "drive-thru" situation, isolating cars getting a fill up from those passing on the street. Glass-topped pumps advertised automotive wares.

With the flourishing middle-class increasingly ensconced in a flourishing number of automobiles, it soon became apparent that they had few places to go. Henry Ford's dream of a family enjoying "hours of pleasure in God's great open spaces" couldn't happen without roads—preferably roads that were well marked and adequately paved.

Transportation activists conceived of the Lincoln Highway in 1912 as a way of making the automotive age a reality. By 1913 the Lincoln Highway Association had mapped the coast-to-coast route and by 1914 the "road" was a reality. The highway bisected the middle of the nation—a hodgepodge of some thirty-three hundred miles encompassing everything from swathes of newly paved macadam (in showplace areas) to eighteenth-century turnpikes and wagon-rutted dirt roads.

Prior to the Lincoln Highway, roads often did not connect: many just petered out in remote barnyards. Few people had any idea about roads ten or twenty miles beyond where they lived. Small wonder there were fewer than 150 transcontinental trips recorded in 1913. These great adventures were acts of faith and fostered a sense of community on the open road. In spirit, they were not far removed from the courageous treks of settlers in wagon trains fifty or a hundred years before.

"I don't miss the old roads too much, but there was a different sort of camaraderie then, and many would stop to help a stranded motorist or give a lift to a hitchhiker."

—Robert Dekker, Palos Heights, Illinois

"... as we approached each other, we would stop right in the middle of the road and exchange road information, and maybe talk for a few minutes—there wasn't much traffic. If you met someone from your state you would pull over and visit for awhile."

—Herbert Reitker, Sr., La Mirada, California

"The interstates are great but I still prefer the old U.S. highways. That's the way it is with old travelers like me—we like the little towns, small town people, and 'The Way it Wuz.'"

—Adrian J. Gebhart, Detroit, Michigan

The white-on-white color scheme on this 1907 Thomas Touring is rather sedate, but the Thomas was something of a performance car in its day. A Thomas Flyer set a world record in 1907 by traveling 997 miles in 24 hours. The company slogan was, "You Can't Go By a Thomas, So Go Buy One."

Above: 1907 Ford Model K Touring detail
Left: 1903 Ford Rear Entrance Tonneau detail
Opposite: 1914 Simplex Speed Car

Opposite: 1911 Crane Simplex 4-Passenger Tourabout

This 1914 Model T Roadster dates from the beginning of the Ford legend. Already Ford's dictum of function over form is obvious. The round barn in the background reflects the same utilitarian philosophy: it was built in Oklahoma by a Dutch immigrant who thought the round shape would be resistant to wind storms. So far so good.

Crossing America's wide open spaces in one's trusty 1922 Ford Model T Runabout was not a trip for the fainthearted.

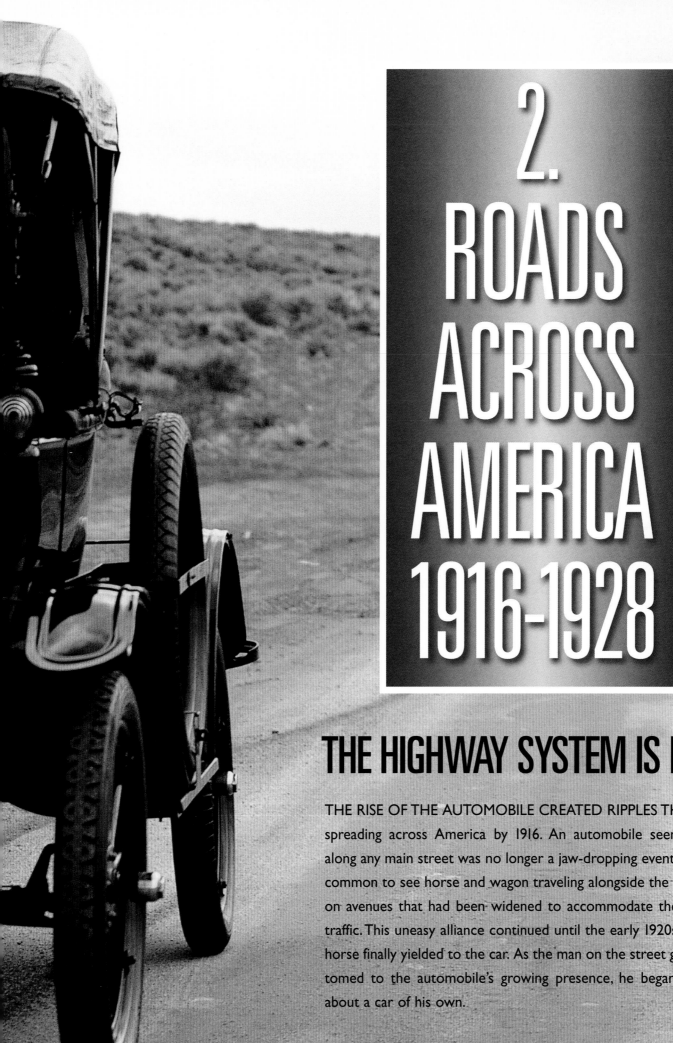

2. ROADS ACROSS AMERICA 1916-1928

THE HIGHWAY SYSTEM IS BORN

THE RISE OF THE AUTOMOBILE CREATED RIPPLES THAT WERE spreading across America by 1916. An automobile seen motoring along any main street was no longer a jaw-dropping event. It was still common to see horse and wagon traveling alongside the automobile on avenues that had been widened to accommodate the increased traffic. This uneasy alliance continued until the early 1920s, when the horse finally yielded to the car. As the man on the street grew accustomed to the automobile's growing presence, he began to dream about a car of his own.

The 1919 Ford Model T Touring is an American classic, and one of the most popular family cars of all time.

The culture and art during this period did much to enhance the dream of automotive ownership. Heralding the machine age, a new aesthetic evolved featuring the machine-conscious art of Cubism and Futurism, even revealed in the billboard art seen by the public. The new "moving picture shows" frequently featured cars, and especially cars with movie stars. Detroit and Hollywood smoothly entered into a cooperative relationship that would continue for many years.

In Europe, the automobile remained an item for the elite, but in America cars became democratized. Mass-production techniques coupled with readily available labor made the automobile affordable by the mid-1920s. America's growing industrialization brought new jobs and increasing wealth to an ever-wider social stratum, thus making the car more accessible in America than Europe. Selling cars to the newly minted middle classes was an article of faith for Henry Ford, the patriarch of America's automotive growth.

At first, proud new car owners were content to join the passing parade on Main Street. Soon, however, the lust for adventure began to unfurl on wings of its own. What lay beyond the outskirts of town? In the 1920s, it became a national pastime for families to explore the countryside on Sunday drives.

These simple journeys spawned the idea of cross-country trips. Although they could have taken the train (the dominant form of transport at the time), many travelers preferred the challenge of the highway (or lack thereof). Americans didn't necessarily need to travel cross-country in their cherished cars, but they simply couldn't resist trying. As a result, the American landscape began to adapt to the automobile just as the automobile adapted itself to the landscape. Families loaded their vehicles and set off into the great unknown filled with a sense of exhilaration:

"It was 1927, and my adventurous parents were busy planning to drive our 1926 Oldsmobile from Oklahoma City to Santa Monica in June. There were no highway maps as we know them. Directions were published by auto clubs. These diagrams showed mileage and landmarks, such as 'at 27 miles turn right at the white school house.'

On the appointed day the four of us, which included me at 14 and my brother 8 years younger, set out. Our first 10 miles were paved; the next hard surface would be 280 miles away at Amarillo. Asphalt had replaced the old plank road through the sands of the Mojave Desert. This was a disappointment since I would have relished the excitement of riding the planks. These were scarcely wide enough to accommodate a car. Should you have the misfortune of letting a wheel go over the edge, other drivers would have to lift you back in order to continue their journey."

—Robert C. Scott, Los Angeles, California

Left:
With growing public awareness of the automobile, the advertising image became crucial to new car sales. The first brand to capitalize on this phenomenon was the Jordan, which thrived on the motto "Somewhere, West of Laramie." This meant drivers could depend on Jordans like this 1923 Playboy to traverse the open spaces of the American West. This simple motto enticed a generation of consumers to take the plunge.

A true "land yacht" on wheels, the 1916 Crane-Simplex Touring is loaded with nautical styling cues: note the ship-styled air ducts on the car's front end and the propeller attaching the spare tire to the rear. The unique design can be traced to the owner's occupation: Mr. Henry Crane built marine engines.

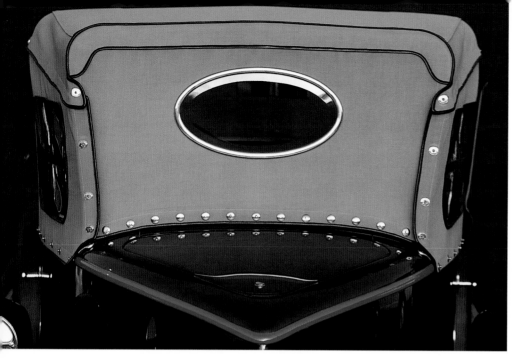

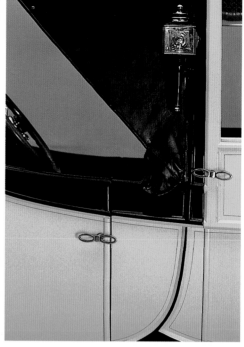

1927 Stutz Black Hawk Speedster   *1927 Lincoln Coaching Brougham detail*

By necessity, the most basic transformation of our landscape was caused by the construction of roads. Starting out with cow paths and rutted trails, we progressed to plank roads and at long last had the macadam road. We carved up the countryside in pursuit of the mechanical magic carpet ride. The demand for viable highways became critical as automobiles—particularly the Model T—proliferated.

The Lincoln Highway broadened travel opportunities for coast-to-coast travelers, but those wishing to journey to the Southwest still struggled against many odds. Highway authorities mapped Route 66 in 1926 by stringing together the National Old Trails Roads to form a continuous ribbon of blacktop from Lake Michigan to Southern California's Pacific Ocean. It was years, however, until the new road was completely paved.

Prior to the completion of the "Main Street of America" and the rise of its corresponding roadside businesses, the auto traveler frequently depended upon the fabled "kindness of strangers" in making his way across the land:

"Outside of Holbrook, Arizona, I helped a woman change a tire. When I was finished, she went to the back of her pickup and cut me a piece of homemade apple pie. I told her I'd follow her into Holbrook, and as I drove by, she waved to me and I could read her lips saying thanks a lot."

—Herbert Reitker, Sr., La Mirada, California

As roadways spun their tenuous web across the country, more and more Americans hit the road armed only with their daring spirit and a few provisions. Roadside businesses quickly sprung up to cater to the traveler. The new gas stations and garages serviced their mechanical conveyances while tourist cabins offered shelter to passengers weary from long travel over bumpy roads.

1928 Packard Convertible Coupe: wheel details (top and bottom), and door handle detail (center).

"An innovation for auto travelers had arisen—the 'tourist camp.' These generally were comprised of a dozen single-walled frame cabins with one or two double beds, renting for a dollar or one fifty, respectively. These had no bedding, only mattresses. We carried ours in duffel bags lashed to the car's running boards. A latrine for all guests was placed in the middle of the camp. Water was supplied by a spigot at the door of each cabin. Sometimes a gas or kerosene plate was available for cooking. The final amenity was a broom. This almost always had to be used before unpacking since the former occupant had been too rushed to perform the task."

—Robert C. Scott, Los Angeles, California

Major technological innovations almost always require early users to be their own mechanics. With the Internet paving the way for the twenty-first century, many of us struggle daily to configure and interface our computers with the new cyber-reality. Similarly, a cross-country automotive trip during the 1920s required the driver to be his own mechanic. Assistance was not always available, forcing early road warriors to rely on their own abilities.

"My experience dates back to 1920, at which time I was twelve years old. Our family transportation was limited to streetcars and trains. My father reached the point in his life where he thought we should have some family transportation. His choice was a 1920 Harley Davidson motorcycle with a sidecar attached. Mother's seat was in the sidecar. Brother Dick sat on a little stool between Mother's sprattled legs, which left his head just a little above the front panel of the sidecar. My seat was on a tandem behind my Father.

Dad had rigged up a luggage carrier on the back of the side car, which accommodated picnic food and a small propane gas stove. Food never tasted so good!

On one memorable trip to Eureka, we experienced a flat tire on the rear of the motorcycle. Removing the rear wheel and repairing the puncture bordered on a major project, and I think it was responsible to help my dad make up his mind to trade the motorcycle for a shiny new 1925 Chevrolet sedan."

—Art J. Mueller, St. Louis, Missouri

Below: This 1928 Chevrolet Pickup was marketed under the Chevrolet slogan "Bigger and Better." What could be more American? Chevrolet's 6-cylinder engine was indeed larger than Ford's 4-cylinder model. The slogan paid off: 1928 was the second year in a row that Chevrolet was #1 in sales.

Opposite: In 1902, water was the dominant medium for cooling a car engine. It still is. But H. H. Franklin and engineer John Wilkinson thought they had a better idea—air. The Franklin Motor Company produced only air-cooled engines from 1902 until its demise in 1934. The stately lines of this 1924 Franklin Series 10C was an attempt by the company to reassure a public skeptical of this unusual method. Pioneering aviators Charles Lindbergh and Amelia Earhart understood the physics of air cooling well, and they favored the Franklin. But it was all a lost cause: eventually, Franklin was forced to cobble on a fake radiator in order to placate the customer. This model features wooden wheels and frame with an aluminum body.

In the early days, motoring could be a risky proposition, making a drive of any duration a matter of faith. Consequently, early service stations were often designed like temples to impart faith in their service, just as banks used classical architecture to impart faith in the financial system. Earl Eckel copied this dramatic 1922 Greek Revival design for Guy's Filling Station in Washington, New Jersey, from a station in Florida. Equally reflective of motoring's stalwart spirit in the early days are the upright lines of this 1927 Willys-Knight Great Six Varsity Roadster. Resulting from a collaboration between the Willys-Overland company and engineer Charles Knight, the Willys-Knight featured the so-called Silent Knight engine. Only 3 Varsity Roadsters are known to have survived, perhaps because not every community has a service station of Guy's caliber.

3.
DEPRESSION AND SALVATION
1929-1940

CAR CULTURE IN THE 1930s

IRONICALLY, THE 1929 STOCK MARKET CRASH DID NOT deter Detroit from turning out automobiles in ever greater numbers. That year the Ford Model A made its debut along with the popular six-cylinder "Stovebolt" Chevrolet. Although automobiles were more affordable, they remained a luxury—a hard choice for many to make. Many people, it turned out, were willing to make sacrifices to own a car—the clothing industry complained that people did without new clothes so they could buy and maintain an automobile; others cut back on food expenses.

Designed by Gordon Buehrig for an honorary fireman, George Whittell, this 1933 Duesenberg Model SJ features a black-and-white paint job of unparalleled sophistication. The two-tone scheme accentuates the sculptural beauty of the hand-wrought Duesenberg body and attracted ample attention when Mr. Whittell drove it in parades.

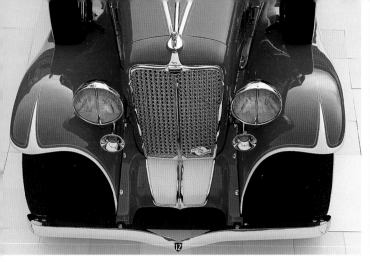

1932 Auburn Cabriolet V-12 detail   1935 Brewster Convertible detail

Aiding in their decision was an advertising industry that was coming of age, honing its skills at promoting the car as key to a better life for mass-market buyers. Practicality was a persuasive rationale for buying an automobile: cars had an important role ferrying folks to school and work and toting the groceries home. But cars also assumed a social role as families took drives after supper to "cool off" on hot summer evenings instead of relaxing on their front porches. Going for a car ride became popular entertainment. Some saw it as a threat to moral standards when "courting" moved from the family parlor to the back seat. Preachers disdained the "all day Sunday trip" that lured families from church pew to highway.

Every weekend, rain or shine, summer or winter, Helen Tobias Martin and her family traveled from St. Louis to Sullivan, Missouri:

"My first trip on 66 was in '29 in a touring car with side curtains. A few times, I remember starting out in the morning and not arriving till late afternoon—a matter of about 80 miles. Sometimes I sat between dad and Uncle Joe. Dad played the harmonica, we all sang, and the men always had a crock with 'home brew.' We always stopped at the Diamonds for gas and popcorn coming and going. We would pull over just outside of St. Clair city limits. We would split open a watermelon and eat under the shade of this big oak tree—no speeding cars—no nothing."

—Helen Tobias Martin, Sullivan, Missouri

The miracle during this period may not have been the automobile, but rather the highway system that developed to support it. Although America developed a plan for a national highway system in 1925, it was almost 1940 before the dream became a reality and the highways were paved from coast to coast. Once a network of through-roads was in place, America suddenly became smaller. What happened "over there" was no longer unknowable—you could go see for yourself if you were so inclined. And so they were: growing numbers of motorists took to exploring the highways beyond their city limits.

In the spring of 1929, the Grider family of four traveled from southwest Missouri to California on a 1929 Harley Davidson motorcycle with a double-passenger sidecar:

"Route 66 was unpaved all the way. It took us seven days to reach Los Angeles at a total cost of $35. Campgrounds sometimes cost 25 cents; at times, we just camped by the road. [The] wife and I and children

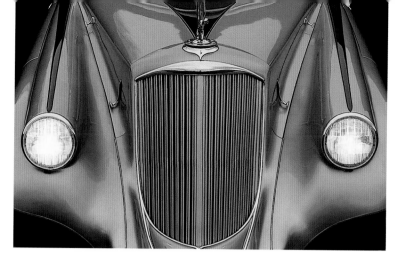

1933 Pierce Arrow Silver Arrow Front detail

ages 3½ and 1 year, took the following provisions and bought no food on the way: a 7' × 7' umbrella tent, 4 camp stools, washtub & board, 2-burner gas stove for cooking and heat, 2 bedrolls, ½ gal. ice cream freezer, 2 water bags, kerosene lantern for light, pressure cooker, aluminum kettle packed with pots, coffee pot & tableware, grocery box containing whole home-grown ham, flour, meal, eggs, jellies, Pet canned milk for gravy and bread making, and summer and winter clothing for four. With the heavy load, the [Harley] would run 50 MPH in high gear. I could out-run Greyhound buses on the dirt, washboard road. Most cars of that day could hardly make the grade at Oatman Pass northeast of Needles, California, but the cyclin' Griders made it in 2nd gear fully loaded."

—John Grider, Greenfield, Missouri

The roaring twenties only roared for a small percentage of people at the top. In the heartland, growing industrialization forced farmers (particularly in the Midwest) either to mechanize their operations or sell out. Those unable to afford the new farm technology moved off the farms to find work elsewhere. Many found jobs servicing the burgeoning numbers traversing Route 66.

Once-lonely roadsides soon became hot beds of commercial activity. The vital trinity of gas, food, and lodging were inevitably the first enterprises to open their doors. Budding entrepreneurs figured it would be nice to have a bite to eat or maybe spend the night while your car was being serviced. Service stations evolved from curbside pumps in front of the general store into freestanding full-service entities along the highway; the visible gas pumps of the 1920s gave way to the "calculating pumps" of the 1930s.

Diners and cafés became popular destinations for so-called home-cooked meals. Roadside lodgings—the first were campgrounds—sprang up in close proximity to the new service stations and cafés. Most of these enterprises were family operations, almost always paid for in cash and expanded slowly, as more cash became available. As proprietors prospered, the campground, for example, evolved into a tourist camp featuring cabins. Everyone worked: mothers and grandmothers cleaned, children tended fires to heat bath water, and dads and granddads built new cabins.

In many cases, the services surrounding the roads outclassed the roads themselves. Rich and poor drivers alike raised a clamor for more roads and better driving conditions. Highways held the promise of business opportunity for those less endowed, and the very wealthy, with their fabulous coach-built cars, felt stymied by the roads of the early 1930s.

1930 DuPont Royal Town Car detail

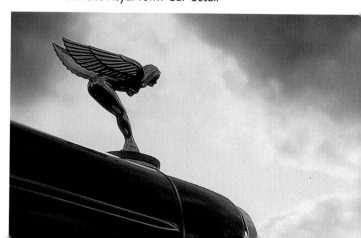

A pristine example of the Victorian-style structures built to serve American railroads in their heyday, this depot is located in Galena, Kansas. These days the depot serves as a Mining and Historical Museum, commemorating the days when Galena was a mining boomtown for lead and zinc. During the boom Galena was served by no less than three separate railroad lines. Ironically, the 1931 Model A Ford helped replace the railroads as America's primary form of public transportation: Americans preferred the individuality of driving to the schedule of trains. So eagerly awaited was the Model A (the successor to Ford's top-selling Model T) that police were called out on its arrival to restrain curious crowds in a number of cities. With a reasonable $475 price tag and 4 cylinders pumping 40 horsepower, the Model A helped Ford stay on top of the market.

Below: Kaveney's Pharmacy, with its bright red ceramic facade, was the centerpiece of town in the days when tiny Wilmington, Illinois, was struggling to establish itself. With the suburban migration, times changed, but Kaveney's was saved by owners who turned it into an antique emporium. The 1931 Chrysler Sport Roadster was also a case where tough times led to a memorable design. Contending with the Depression, Chrysler had to create the most seductive possible car. Designers took inspiration from the Cord L-29 luxury sedan and scored big with this roadster's racy, low-slung styling and a straight-8 engine. Like Kaveney's, this roadster has survived because its classic original design earned the care and attention of preservation-minded owners.

Right: For early-morning empire builders, Lou Mitchell's restaurant offers a breakfast of champions that has made it a Chicago legend. Just a few blocks from the origin of Route 66, Lou Mitchell's has seen many travelers filling up prior to the continental crossing. There is also a solid clientele of traders and other denizens of the nearby Chicago Board of Trade and Mercantile Exchange. This spectacular 1937 Cord 812 Supercharged Phaeton would be the ride of choice for a successful financier. Designed in 1936 by renowned stylist Gordon Buehrig, the Phaeton was revolutionary in its streamlined design and boisterous power. Mounted on the Cord's dash is a plaque guaranteeing that this particular model will go 110.8 MPH. Truly a car for the City of the Big Shoulders, the Cord's Lycoming Supercharged V-8 engine, with 289 cubic inches and front-wheel drive, made it the fastest stock car produced prior to 1947.

SELECTED NO1
BREAKFAST
& LUNCH
RESTAURANT
IN AMERICA
Mitchell's
Serving the worl
finest COFFEE
This is Lou Mitchell's
RESTAURANT
& BAKERY
We do our own
Quality baking
Hand Made
Milk Duds
BAKER
565

Opposite: Erret Loban Cord was a wheeler-dealer who enjoyed working the stock market as much as he did the design and manufacture of automobiles. In the automotive world, Cord remains one of America's most influential designers. He created his self-named company in the late 1920s to fill the gap between his medium-priced Auburn line and the top-flight Duesenberg. The Cord L-29 pictured here was one of the first cars ever built with front-wheel drive. This feature catapulted Cord to the forefront of automotive innovation. As is often the case with engineering breakthroughs, certain shortcomings became apparent. The car was slower than hoped for and handling was a little skittish in adverse conditions. Compensating for mechanical faults were the L-29's movie-star looks. Front-wheel drive allowed for a low, flowing style that made the Cord one of the most attractive cars of its own decade and any since.

This back-seat bar in a 1930 Cadillac limousine is the last word in luxury. Not only were cut-crystal decanters provided as standard equipment for this mobile watering hole—they also included crystal perfume atomizers that riders could use to freshen up after imbibing.

Ironically, America was turning out some of history's finest and most elegant automobiles at a time when road conditions made driving them at speed capacity dangerous if not impossible. Imagine driving a Ferrari or a Porsche today within a strict 30-MPH speed limit imposed not by police, but by the physical limitations and dangers of the corduroy roads that are your only option!

Curiously, the Great Depression fueled the growth of roadside America. Paving the highway system provided ready work for the hordes of unemployed: the government allocated funds from the Works Progress Administration in order to keep the maximum number of people working throughout the 1930s. WPA funds helped pave the entire length of Route 66 and other key arteries across the country. Route 66 carried some destitute families to lands of greater opportunity; the paving of roads gave work to many that stayed behind.

Most of the early road construction was done with animals. Teams of mules pulled split logs that graded the road before paving. There was little or no money to build bridges, so the states would finish their highways by pouring concrete through the washes. In addition to the usual mechanical difficulties, the motorist had to contend with the possibility of quicksand when the washes were flowing, or—even worse—flash floods:

"In 1933, while driving a Model A Ford, the constant shaking loosened a jet in the carburetor and gasoline poured out of the bottom. I couldn't find the lost jet, but [I] fashioned a plug out of cork to stop the leak. Somehow the car ran with the cork plug as well as with the jet. On the same trip, near Gallup, New Mexico, about 200 feet of the road was under water as the result of a flash flood. Several cars were lined up at each side of the underwater portion. An Indian on horseback was nearby. I gave him a quarter to ride through before me so I could judge the depth of the water. At one point the water was so deep that the fan belt threw water on the spark plugs, which then shorted out. After drying them, I threw a flannel shirt over them to keep them dry. We finally made it safely with the other cars following me."

—William H. Shallenberger, Oxnard, California

1930 Franklin Pursuit Grill

The Packard motto was "Ask The Man Who Owns One," relying on word of mouth to spread the company's reputation for quality. Packard's celebrated Ray Dietrich designed the impressive body of this 1933 Packard V-12 Sport Phaeton.

"Blue skies smilin' at me, Nothing but blue skies do I see . . ." Irving Berlin's 1927 ode to unbridled optimism would be tragically undercut in a few short years by the Great Depression. But for now this 1929 Duesenberg Model J sails blithely on.

Overleaf: 1930 Duesenberg Model J Phaeton

Below: 1936 Duesenberg Model SJ Convertible Coupe wheel detail
Opposite: This elegant gray 1935 Duesenberg Model SSJ is the
definition of a sports car. "SS" stands for "Super-Short": the
car's short wheelbase pares down the typically massive
Duesenberg proportions, making this car more maneuverable
in tight spots. Yet this is still a hefty automobile, with an overall
weight of 5,010 lbs. Only two SSJ's were ever built: Gary Cooper
bought this one, prompting Clark Gable to buy the second.

Elaborate celebrations were staged in towns on the red-letter days when sections of road were completed—bands and parades of cars with mule-driven wagon trains led the way along the new "hard" road. Because it was cheaper to take the bus during the Depression than to drive, buses developed as a new transportation industry. Trucks began hauling goods across the roadway too. The road and the automobile became important as an escape route for destitute farmers leaving behind a rain-starved Midwest and as a living for those who worked along the highway. The Dust Bowl exodus chronicled so vividly by John Steinbeck in *The Grapes of Wrath* broke the hearts of those leaving their homes and those watching them go. Route 66 bore witness to the everyday traumas of the Okies. New roadside entrepreneurs had to cope with indigent families asking for work to buy a tank of gas or loaf of bread. Many shop owners bought items they didn't need or simply extended credit to help them along their way to California—the land of milk and honey. Years later a traveler recalls the generosity of a shopkeeper:

"In 1936, our family of five left Milford, Nebraska. We had a 1929 Model A Ford and an 18' trailer/mobile home that a neighbor and I had built.... [At Amarillo,] we had eaten everything edible, so we gave ourselves a treat and ate at the local café. Meals were $.35 each, and coffee was $.90 to fill the jug. [The] local store had no snacks, but the owner did give us a bag of dried apples for a dollar."

On the way to Albuquerque ... "This was the worst of all the roads, complete with mountains that went straight up and then straight down. On one, before getting to Albuquerque, we almost didn't get to the top. Low gear and slipping the tired clutch put us over. Then at a curve on the downside (we were going 35 MPH in low), there was a group of bandits stretched across the road to stop us, but our screaming engine scared them away. At the California line we got our sticker and welcome to California brochure. We were just another 'Okie,' and there were many of us. Wow! We had arrived. After making it over the final pass, we started to see orange groves. All you could drink for $.10! Thompson grapes for $.10 a peck! Love this place!"

—Jay Bannister, Rosamond, California

Henry Ford's automobile company grew like wildfire on the popularity of the Model T, but it almost lost its leadership position due to Ford's infamous resistance to change. The competition gained on Ford by producing models that made the words "Model T" a synonym for "old fashioned." At last Ford conceded to pressure and turned out the Model A just in time for the Depression. The Model A's designer— Henry's son, Edsel—included some Lincoln styling details that gave the Model A an upscale appearance despite its thrifty price tags. The Model A was an instant success—its relative austerity squared perfectly with the tough realities of the Depression. The Model A was available in a variety of body types, but the 2-door Deluxe Phaeton shown here had a very limited production run. This was one of the first cars to feature vacuum-operated windshield wipers as standard equipment.

As America shook off the Depression, the fallout from tough economic times caused many automobile manufacturers to cease production. Ironically, the automobile industry staggered just as roadside America was taking off. The roadside boom began with more and more establishments to service the car—gas stations running the gamut from the streamlined architectural designs of major oil companies to independent dealers hawking the cheapest gas available. These service stations lavished attention upon the customer. A fleet of uniformed attendants raced to "service" your car: fill the tank, clean your windshield, check the water in your radiator, check your tire pressure—even empty your ashtray.

Gas stations proliferated, launching the race to attract the motorist's attention. Promotional giveaways, uniforms, and service quality became increasingly important factors in shaping the motorist's decision of where to stop. Gas stations, cafés, motels, and tourist attractions assumed a larger-than-life visibility in order to attract the passing motorist's attention. Buildings often became a giant version or advertisement of the product sold, such as a hot dog stand in the form of a giant hot dog. This pop architecture style—known as programmatic architecture—reached its heyday in the 1950s, although it was used with less frequency into the 1970s. Fast-food franchises originated in the mid-1930s with the Steak 'n Shake stand in St. Louis, Missouri. The little stand expanded into a mighty chain of coveted hamburger stands across the Midwest.

Roadside signs became vitally important, causing a demand for sign painters along the highway. The painter's handicraft pointed out features on a motel, restaurant, or gas station that were unique to their establishment—clean rest rooms, a coffee shop and homemade biscuits, even radio. The first Burma Shave billboard series appeared in Minnesota in 1925: by the late 1930s the billboard series concept became vitally important along Route 66.

Unlike eastern states, with their preexisting urban centers, the western states were a tabula rasa. They were entirely free to invent their own mythology along the new highways. Route 66 crossed some of the most romantic countryside in America. It soon became clear that for roadside entrepreneurs in the Southwest, the cowboys and Indians motif could be milked all the way to the bank. "Spend the night in a teepee" read the popular billboard promoting the famed Wigwam Motel. Powwows and Indian jewelry helped tribes along the route trade much-needed supplies. It was a good deal for the Indians who lived in the area and the tourists: Indian jewelry and crafts became prized purchases of travelers through the region.

Top: This is the famous "coffin nose" of the 1937 Cord Convertible designed by Gordon Buehrig.
Bottom: 1937 Cord Model 812 Berline Limousine dashboard

Right: The 1937 Cord Model 812 Berline Limousine was built for speed and this glorious strip of two-lane blacktop is just the place to see how fast she'll go.

Despite the Southwest's roadside allures and the cosseting of paved roads, there was still one great hurdle that put fear into the heart of every motorist through the region—the Mojave Desert. Constance Rimkus and her family crossed the Mojave in 1940:

"We had to cross it and it was hot as *%&*#>. There was a big sign that said 'Fill your gas tank here. Last station before going through the desert.' So we stopped and filled the tank and after that asked the attendant if we all could have a glass of water. We were so thirsty and it was so hot! He said, 'Sure, for twenty-five cents a glass, you can drink all you want.' We went into total shock. We asked, 'You're charging us for water? You can't do that, water is free!' He said, 'Oh yes I can. Do you see any other place around here where you can get any water?' Of course not. We were virtually in the middle of nowhere. Not another house or barn or store could be seen anywhere. He reminded us that we might have a flat tire and the strength to change it could make people faint. Plus he also reminded us we should carry water on the front of the car in a canvas bag to cool the hot air blowing across the radiator. So all in all he got us for quite a bundle. Oh yes, he also sold us a thermos bottle full of water. His parting words to us were, 'I hope you folks make it. So many don't, ya know.'"

—Constance M. Rimkus, Hickory Hills, Illinois

1937 Studebaker Coupe Express detail

1921 Pierce Arrow detail

1930 Packard Model 7-34 Speedster Runabout detail

1930 Graham Paige All Weather Cabriolet detail

1940 Packard Custom Station Wagon detail

Wild tales of murder, mayhem, tortured Indian spirits, and buried treasure continue to haunt Two Guns, Arizona, located between Flagstaff and Winslow. Once Route 66 was certified, these myths were powerful enough to prompt the opening of a genuine tourist trap at Two Guns featuring a wild animal zoo, curio shop, and gas station, which later burned down in a mysterious fire. A straight-8 Ford engine powers this 1935 Ford Pickup, which stands in front of the long-gone "Mountain Lions" cage of Two Guns's wild animal zoo. This 1935 Ford half-ton Pickup dates from the era when Henry Ford's reign over the American automobile market was on the wane. Chrysler and GM were nipping at the aging Ford's heels, but the addition of the V-8 engine gave Ford a burst of speed that lasted to the end of World War II.

Opposite, above: Automotive designer Harley Earl was selected to design the LaSalle, a new GM division positioned to fill the price gap between Buick and the upscale Cadillac. His final design won Earl kudos, with the fender and radiator grill clearly influenced by Hispano-Suiza designs of the day.

In 1938, Arlene Donnell's Aunt Bridget took her to California for her high school graduation gift.

"Aunt Bridget was 4'11" at full stretch, weighing 90 pounds. She was an excellent driver with a passion for big cars. She had a new four-door, bright-red De Sota, and into this we all climbed. Bridget drove the entire trip with a big pillow at her back so she could reach the clutch and brakes. I sat in the middle of the front seat (straddling the gearshift) guarding our travel book. In the middle of the back seat was Mom (grandmother)—an ample woman—Pennsylvania Dutch background. At her feet was a massive wooden 'FOOD BOX' with supplies to sustain the 6 of us the entire trip. Mom was convinced that no food would be available in the wilds of the west, so she was prepared to feed us. She maintained strict control over that box and could produce snacks, sandwiches, cookies, fruit, etc., upon request. I marvel at the amount of stuff she managed to cram into that wooden crate. Somewhere in New Mexico or Arizona, there was an infestation of crickets. In order to keep them off the highway, cricket fences had been built beside the road. These were metal pens filled with crude oil or creosote. The crickets were mounded waist or shoulder high and the stench was overpowering. Now in Mom's cornucopia food box were some cantaloupes. These had ripened in the heat. The air inside that red De Sota was redolent with over-ripe cantaloupe—the outside heavy with dead crickets in oil. It was many years before I could even think about muskmelons. The California boarder had a checkpoint. We were searched to be certain we carried no fruit into the state. I gladly parted with the cantaloupes. The border guard, looking into that big red De Sota filled with bleary-eyed Missourians, greeted us with "Welcome to SUNNY California." Mom called him all manner of Dutch names, because he had taken some of her precious vittles."

—Arlene C. Donnell, Springfield, Missouri

Opposite, below: Packard first offered air-conditioning—called Packard Weather Conditioning—for the first time in its 1940 models, including this Packard 110 Convertible. Air-conditioning remained a prized luxury option until the 1960s. One can only imagine how prized it might have been to the occupants of this car traveling amid the desert heat encircling this Arizona trading post.

Left: Boyd Coddington transformed this 1933 Ford into a modern-day hot rod. Inspired by the souped-up cars of the 1950s, Coddington caters to the men who have made their fortune yet still dream of cruisin' à la American Graffiti. With the flame motif blazing back from the hood and state-of-the-art mechanics below it, this baby is ready to burn up any street in the nation.

Above: This revamped 1932 Ford Roadster is one of the original Mean Machines. The hot-rod movement sprung up in the 1950s in Southern California where building your own personal fire-breathing monster made you a bona fide "hep cat."

The telephone poles along this flat stretch of road in California's Central Valley roll by in endless procession. Residents in such country often opt for transportation that contrasts with the landscape, as is certainly the case with this revamped red-hot 1934 Ford Coupe.

The boxy shape and warm woodwork of this 1929 Ford Model A Station Wagon make it look a little like a garden shed on wheels. Many of these workhorse Ford station wagons were used as farm vehicles.

With its fluid ivory hood and golden wood sides, this 1940 Packard Custom Station Wagon is the perfect car for the gentleman farmer. The wood sides proclaim an affinity with the earth while the meticulous grace of the limousine-like hood could pass muster at any gathering of automotive thoroughbreds.

The front end of this 1939 Chrysler Imperial
Station Wagon has the feel of a grand touring
car while the wood paneling of the rear
gives the car a friendly, approachable feeling.
This car is just right for a family interested
in seeing the world in style.

Above: Close to the Edge, Marin Headlands, California
Right: Grand Canyon Rail Stop, Williams, Arizona

Grand Canyon Hotel, Williams, Arizona

Angel's Barber Shop, Seligman, Arizona

Ed's Camp, Mojave Desert, Arizona

Left: 1947 Studebaker Pickup Truck, Tucumcari, New Mexico
Above: Truckin', Two Guns, Arizona

Hollywood diner, Grant, New Mexico

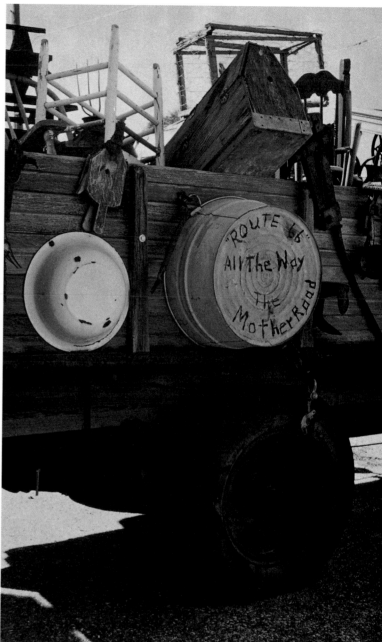

Dustbowl truck, Amarillo, Texas

Opposite: Two-lane blacktop, New Mexico

In 1967, T. J. Otcasek and his new bride set off for a dream honeymoon in California in their new 1967 Cadillac Eldorado. "What better way to start our new life together? ... About 15 miles east of Grants, [New Mexico], we came upon the most beautiful ribbons of cement we had seen so far. Blue sky, majestic mountains, new bride, new Eldo, and a ribbon of cement as far as you could see. Not too difficult to figure out now was the time to let her go (the Eldo, that is)."

T. J. Otcasek,
Pueblo West, Colorado

Above: Lucille's Gas, Hydro, Oklahoma

Left: Britten Water Tower
And you thought all the leaning towers were in Pisa. In a con-
summate piece of high-plains architectural theater, the Britten
water tower was deliberately created with one leg shorter than
the others. As it is the only structure on the horizon, approaching
motorists become fascinated by the irregularity, eventually ques-
tioning the very tilt of the horizon itself. This 1930 Ford Model A
Flatbed truck is immune to the joke as it continues about its
daily tasks with relentless purpose. Owned by the local propri-
etors of the Truck Terminal and Ranch House Café, this Model A
has a history of hard work for its previous owners—it was first
used to haul boilers off the oil fields, then to haul grain.

4. RETOOLING FOR THE BOOM 1941-1950

"1942. LITTLE DID WE KNOW THAT ROUTE 66 AND OUR WAY of life would disappear, never to return. World War II had been declared, and all the young men had either gone into the service or were expecting to go. We were two young people, married for a short time and trying to squeeze in all the adventure we could. We decided to go to California, packed up our black Ford V-8 and away we went . . . We loved every mile and stopped at every pig-path . . . We made it over the mountain and sailed into San Bernardino. Those beautiful palm trees and the orange groves! This was all over 50 years ago. My darling husband died and I can no longer talk about this with him. But it is inscribed in my memory, never to fade away."

—Jane S. Neal, Greenwood, Indiana

After the war, America's industries began retooling for civilian production. One of the first fruits of this industrial transformation was this all-new 1948 Studebaker Commander Coupe. Surrounded by its own "retooling" equipment and automotive paraphernalia, this is a machine in its element. As memorable as the car is the garage that surrounds it—a male bastion reflecting the mechanical skills and collecting habits of its owner. The Commander's styling is still fresh, reflecting the dynamic influence of famed designers Raymond Loewy, Virgil Exner, and their then-young apprentice, Robert E. Bourke. Exner would later go on to design the Chrysler masterpieces of the 1950s.

Opposite: The solid construction of Cadillacs made them popular for traversing the long distances of the American West as well as the civilized boulevards back East. This 1941 Cadillac Series 60 was a stout ship for the uncharted waters west of the Mississippi.

Overleaf: The toothy grille of this 1948 Buick Roadmaster presents a blinding array of chrome, earning it the moniker "The Million Dollar Grin." It's a little like your fat-cat Uncle Marvin showing off his expensive new bridgework at a family gathering.

With wartime gasoline rationing, traffic and business across the newly paved transcontinental highways slowed to a crawl. Military convoys depended on the highway during this time to move critical wartime parts along major arteries on their way to war. The highways also conveyed manpower for the new aviation industry: many workers and their families drove to California (particularly Southern California), returning in summer months to visit Grandma and Grandpa back home.

A principle source of revenue for some roadside businesses during this period were the military bases. The bases in Las Vegas, for example, spun a steady stream of off-duty defense workers into its casinos and fun palaces. Las Vegas's first motor hotel, El Rancho Vegas, appeared on the scene to entice service men to stop by for some "fun" in the sun-blasted desert. Las Vegas founder Bugsy Siegel anticipated a big postwar boom in fun and gambling, and he hit the jackpot.

By 1942 Detroit was not building any cars: America had redirected all its mighty industries to the war effort. Consumers had money (unlike in the Depression), but wartime rationing left them with nothing to buy. Roadside enterprises accepted ration coupons and struggled long nights to balance their accountings. Servicemen—and families traveling to visit servicemen—were the principal customer base on the road:

"My second trip down '66 was in 1945. My husband and I retraced the [first] route, this time from L.A. to Kentucky . . . As it was shortly after the war, there were many things that were still unavailable. Among these were tires. Because we couldn't buy new tires, we had all four tires recapped, plus the spare. We lost the caps to all five tires. Cars were not air-conditioned so we bought an outside tank that was fastened to the outside of the window and blew air on you. It made so much noise that conversation was impossible . . . and [it] gave everyone the sniffles. Forgetting it was sticking out from the car, we drove too close to a post hitting the air conditioner and breaking the window. After that, we bought a canvas bag in case the car overheated or we needed a drink of water. We tied it to the handle of the door on the driver's side. After a few miles, we discovered that the bag had swung back and forth and the metal top of the canvas bag had scraped off all the paint on the driver's side door. The trip cost us five tires, a window, and a paint job."

—Robbie Gordon, Glendale, California

Shortcomings of American highways that weren't clear during the war became very clear afterward. For one thing, the highways were too narrow for new postwar car designs. Soon after the war, the

1948 Ford Woody Wagon detail

federal government became involved in a highway project to upgrade inadequate roads in case another war required the movement of goods and servicemen across the country. Dusting off a long-range government planning survey from 1934, highway authorities used it as the basis for the new interstate system. Unfortunately, the interstate system bypassed many small towns that were highlights of Route 66. America's roadside was about to change again.

While American industries retooled for civilian production, the nation enjoyed an interval of simpler joys. One of these was a return to long-distance motoring once gas rationing was eliminated. From the mid- to late 1940s, Martha Oakes and her siblings made several moves between Indiana and Arizona with her dad, who drove a truck, and her mom, who drove the family Packard:

"As we slowly crossed the country on Route 66, I practiced 'speed reading' by never missing a Burma Shave series and learned map reading skills by tracking our trip with a red crayon on the frayed and aging road map. Mother had taught school, and she never completely put away her lesson book. . . . We didn't nap or tease one another, we were too busy listening to Mother as she drove with one hand and pointed and talked with the other . . . We would follow Daddy into a shady glen near a farm. This would be our campsite. Out came the table; little ones were sent to the nearby farm for water, older ones built a campfire and soon a hot meal was shared on our own familiar table with the tablecloth and wildflowers. After breakfast [the next day], the table was cleared and schoolbooks came out for the day's assignments. Book lessons were completed while we drove, when Mother wasn't teaching from the landscape."

—Martha M. Oakes, Orange Park, Florida

Beginning in 1947, and continuing for almost twenty years, Marcia Ainsworth traveled Route 66 between California and Arkansas so that her folks could see their two grandsons and granddaughter. Here's a description of her trip in 1948:

". . . in a Studebaker with the back seat door handles removed, my 200 pound babysitter asleep in the front, my dog sitting on the portable ice chest, drooling down the back of my neck. After that trip, we graduated to station wagons—no air conditioning, but more room. Going 80 miles an hour, my kids are screaming 'You

Right, top: 1950 Cadillac Series 61 Sedan detail
Right, bottom: With its distinctive center head-
light, this 1948 Tucker 4-Door Sedan looks a little
like an alien visitor. Actually, the Tucker was a bril-
liantly designed car, so far ahead of its time that
it fell afoul of the powers that be in Detroit. The
definitive film portrait of automaker Preston
Tucker and the cars he created is Frances Ford
Coppola's Tucker, A Man and His Dream.

promised to stop and let us get a terrapin and you passed it.' Backing
up for miles on a popular highway is not easy, but we got it. Another
time, going through Texas, it rained tiny frogs no bigger than a quarter.
The road was so slick you could hardly drive and [my] kids were howl-
ing 'you're running over them.' The cars got better, the detours fewer
and I got older. But to this day when I hear Nat King Cole's recording
of Route 66, I still feel the excitement and fun of those years."

—Marcia Ainsworth, Laguna Hills, California

Roadside America retooled with the advent of big-time road
advertising. Traders became fiercely competitive for tourist business. Motels and tourist camps soon
featured swing sets and chairs outside. As summer evenings cooled, guests congregated for kids to play
and adults to share the day's travel experience. In the winter, folks might gather around the front office's
potbelly stove to swap stories. Once TV and air-conditioning crept into most rooms, people no longer
socialized. But the modern motel with its private full baths was almost fully formed during this period.

The seeds of commercial vernacular architecture sown in the 1930s began to germinate in the boom
period following the war. Roadside architecture adopted pop art techniques to attract customers to new
car culture icons: drive-in restaurants and movie theaters, gas stations, donut shops, and especially the roadside souvenir stand (a.k.a. tourist trap). Business began to pick up as we roared out of the wartime era:

"It took us a full day to travel from Cincinnati to St. Louis, and another from St. Louis to Joplin. Therefore, we
always stayed overnight in St. Louis in a motel, which was a big adventure. Grandpa always drove an up-to-
date Buick, and we always packed our thermos and lunch for a picnic along the way. It was always my sis-
ter's and my responsibility to watch for the sign for a 'Roadside Table.' Sometimes, we'd just pull off the road
and set up our own card table to eat [on]. Soon it was time to watch for motel signs. Grandma would imme-
diately ask to 'see the room' so she could check the beds and cleanliness. This is something that was done in
the years of the 1940s and early 1950s .... Motels grew larger and added more attractions. But the big excite-
ment came when we began stopping several times before settling on THE motel, asking whether they had a
pool. Now when we packed for the trip, we always made sure we packed our swimsuits."

—Barbara (Worz) Goddard and Nancy (Worz) Neff, Cincinnati, Ohio

1948 Tucker 4-Door Sedan badge

Tucker's advanced engineering is reflected in this rear view of the 1948 Tucker 4-Door Sedan. Its design predates many of the space-age styling motifs that would become common in later decades.

Below: One of the last of the dual-cowl automobiles, this 1941 Chrysler Newport Dual Cowl Phaeton was specially trimmed for its appearance as an Indianapolis Speedway pace car. Cars like this helped create an aura for the entire Chrysler line. Just look at those swooping fenders.

Opposite: This Sinclair station in Odell, Illinois, recalls the vanished pre-franchise era, when gas stations offered more than just gas. In those days, the magic words "fill 'er up" launched a battalion of attendants into action: they would check the oil and clean the windshield as a matter of course, and were ready with knowledgeable advice on a host of mechanical questions. This 1946 Chrysler Royal recalls a similarly genteel era—its optional sun visor greets the viewer as if tipping its hat.

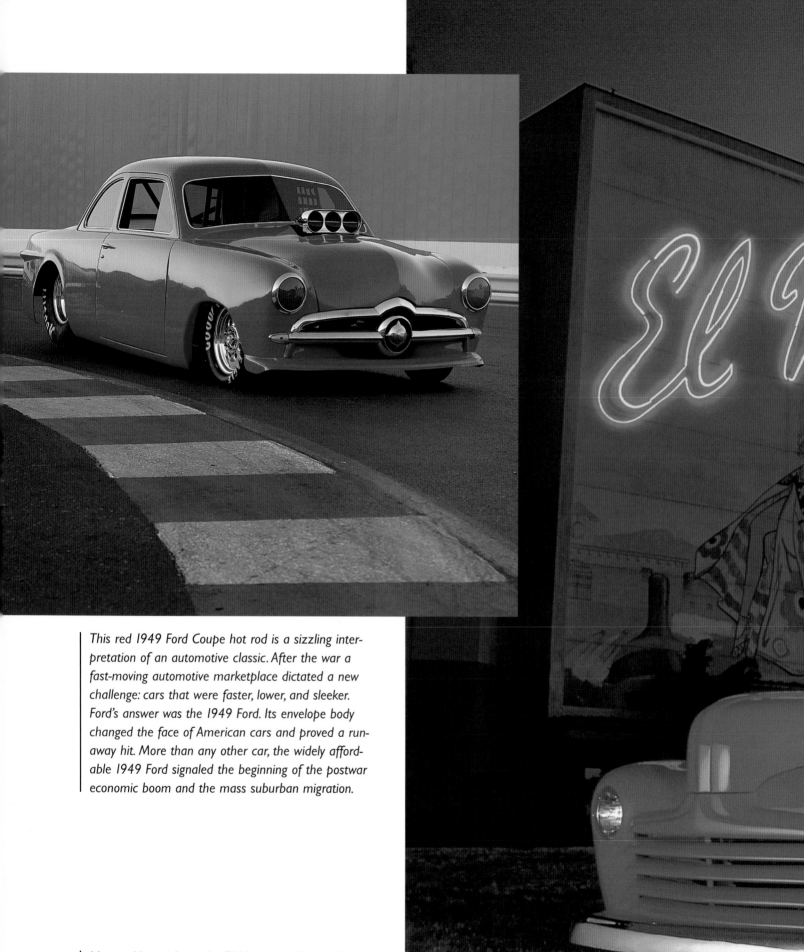

This red 1949 Ford Coupe hot rod is a sizzling interpretation of an automotive classic. After the war a
fast-moving automotive marketplace dictated a new
challenge: cars that were faster, lower, and sleeker.
Ford's answer was the 1949 Ford. Its envelope body
changed the face of American cars and proved a run-
away hit. More than any other car, the widely affordable 1949 Ford signaled the beginning of the postwar
economic boom and the mass suburban migration.

It's a red-hot night at the El Monte, and hot rodders
would often congregate at drive-ins like this to show
off their latest creations. This state-of-the-art 1946
Ford Convertible by Boyd Coddington is right at home.

EL MONTE
DRIVE-IN THEATRE
SHOW STARTS AT DUSK
HOT RODS FROM HELL
GIANT

Blue Swallow
MOTEL
VACANCY
TV
Budget Prices
TRUCK
&
U-HAUL
PARKING
2 for $10
& UP
SCHOOL

Like the spectacular New Mexico desert that surrounds it, the Blue Swallow Motel's pink and red-hot neon draws travelers like an exotic flower. The cool blue of the Swallow logo and gleaming green "refrigerated air" promise cool, clean lodgings in contrast to the blazing desert. Designed in 1942, the Blue Swallow is located in Tucumcari, and was recognized by the National Register of Historic Places as a prime example of early motel design. Equally classic is this ivory white 1949 Chrysler Windsor. Although the car was produced after the war, Chrysler was still retooling for future models. Thus the car reflects the prewar functional design ethnic. For example, the Windsor is designed so gentlemen drivers would not be forced to remove their hats when entering the car. The sun visor and architectural front grille set off the Windsor as a paragon of middle-American respectability.

5.
THE ERA OF FLASH AND FINS
1951-1963

MOTORDOM AND THE MIDDLE CLASS

AFTER THE GREAT DEPRESSION OF THE 1930S AND the wartime rationing of the 1940s, the prevailing mood of the American psyche in the 1950s was feverish delight. Postwar expansion was both an emotional release and a material explosion in production and manufacturing. We had just started to celebrate when the Korean War brought us back to harsh reality. Once that war was over—kaboom!

The glitter gulch of Fremont Street in Las Vegas is a brilliant setting for the top-of-the-line 1959 Cadillac Eldorado Biarritz Convertible Coupe.

In 1946, the gigantic 66 Park-In Theatre in St. Louis, Missouri, opened for business on Route 66. At the time, it boasted the largest drive-in screen in the city, a distinction it held until its demise in 1994. The drive-in theater was devised in a pre–air-conditioned era to provide entertainment on a hot summers' night while the house cooled down. It was a wholesome family activity, with twilight show and playground designed to exhaust the youngsters so more mature folks could enjoy the movie.

During the 1950s, car culture moved into a full tilt boogie: the car dictated our architecture, the way we ate, the way we lived, and the way we drove. Everything was on the move—including us, as we twisted the night away to the electric guitar sounds of Elvis Presley and rock 'n roll. The nonstop monologues of Jack Kerouac and his Beat compatriots summed up our innermost feelings and excitements: go baby go.

Peace and prosperity brought gadgets galore—push-button everything for our ultra-modern utopia. "The Jetsons" didn't come along until the 1960s, but George Jetson's car-that-folds-into-a-briefcase is an innovation that captures the blithe spirit of the 1950s. All these gadgets were designed to part us from our expanding wealth. Americans had more money, which they needed to keep up with those Joneses.

Detroit's dream of selling us a new car every year and putting two cars in every garage became a compelling imperative for many car consumers. Finding ourselves far from home on automotive jaunts, we ate out more often at neon-drenched diners and drive-in restaurants. When at home the rapidly expanding family might enjoy a TV dinner in front of our new TV's. Commercial breaks helped us daydream about our upcoming paid vacations (a lovely innovation of the New Deal) and where we would spend them. Television previewed travel destinations (Disneyland, anybody?) and Detroit churned out fantasy chariots to take us there.

Each year, excited crowds congregated outside auto dealerships to witness the unveiling of the new car models. Detroit carefully choreographed an intricate ensemble of press notices and car shows to fan the flames of "new model fever." GM's traveling Motorama show toured the country each year displaying dream cars—fanciful renditions of the future in metal.

In the early 1950s, automotive design was quite restrained compared to the wacky excess at the decade's end. As the years rolled by, Detroit manufacturers became locked in a fierce competition—an escalating look-at-me design philosophy that was an ironic parallel to the Cold War. Automotive design manifestos were big news and bore ambitious adjectives like *wider, lower, bigger, zoomier.*

One of the most recognizable manifestations of Detroit's escalating design mania was the introduction of tail fins. They grew and grew until they finally culminated in the most outrageous tail fins (the 1959 Cadillac) we have ever seen. It's hard not to see a parallel in the trend toward ample bustlines among 1950s American starlets like Jayne Mansfield when watching those chrome bumpers swell and project during the fifties.

"66"
PARK IN
THEATRE

COMING ATTRACTIONS
ELVIS PRESLEY JAILHOUSE ROCK   SANDRA DEE   A SUMMER PLACE

Right: At Steak 'n Shake, hamburgers are steak burgers and every shake is hand-dipped. Founded in the 1930s with the slogan "in sight it must be right," the Steak 'n Shake chain features steak being ground into hamburger before the eyes of salivating patrons along with a guaranteed wait time of less than 5 minutes. Here, the Springfield, Missouri, Steak 'n Shake hosts the Classic Chevy Club with curbside service.

Who could forget the Colonel in his white suit and black string tie? More importantly, who could forget the bucket of delicious fried chicken he extolled? A large reproduction of that famous bucket spun atop every Kentucky Fried Chicken across America. But look for it today and you'll discover the bucket and the name "Kentucky Fried Chicken" has been replaced with the anonymous acronym KFC: part of an attempt by the cholesterol patrol to make us forget the word fried. As soon as we realized this metamorphosis was occurring, we rushed out to make this photo. We decided the family-sized 1950 Chrysler Town & Country Newport was big enough to hold all the fried chicken we could eat (just barely).

STEAK n SHAKE
SHAKES
GRINDING ONLY GOV'T INSPECTED BEEF FOR STEAKBURGERS
TAKHOMASAK
STEAK n SHAKE
22-313
24-947
MISSOURI
WWW 789
SHOW-ME STATE

The famed Wigwam Village located on Route 66 in Holbrook, Arizona, offers a clean, comfortable night's sleep in a cone-shaped concrete hut. Three Wigwam Villages exist today, all built in the forties and fifties from the original blueprints of architect Frank Redford. His fee? The proceeds from the coin-operated radios located beside every bed. Beside each wigwam, from front to back, are the 1960 Chevrolet Corvette, 1950 Mercury 4-Door Sedan, 1961 Cadillac Series 63, and 1966 Ford Thunderbird.

With all that extra chrome, we needed and got bigger V-8 engines. No doubt about it, the 1950s with their new model designs each year became the American version of a cultural exhibition on wheels. It was the closest the common man saw of art (in action). A day on the road was like a day in a design museum, albeit one with a curator of eccentric taste.

To drive into the future we needed new "modern" four-lane highways with banked curves and EZ On and EZ Off exits. While our new "freeways" were being built, we fumed along on our woefully inadequate two-lane roads behind folks who were slow as cold molasses in January. All that V-8 power and nowhere to really open it up! James Dean in *Rebel Without A Cause* exemplified this decade's frustration at being ready for speed in a world built for slowpokes. Opportunities to pass were eagerly awaited.

Anna Avellino headed to California from New Jersey in 1959 to be with her married daughter and grandchildren. She writes about her life-in-the-fast-lane experiences:

"We were in a row of 5 or 6 cars following a slow truck up a hill. One by one, each car pulled over and passed, so I did the same, only to find a policeman over the hill. He pulled us all over and gave us tickets and directed us to a shack set up like a court and fined us $15 each. I believe this was a tourist trap."

—Anna Avellino, Hesperia, California

Highway congestion caused the road rage virus to multiply in our blood. Yves Bolomet, now deceased, writes about his 1956 two-week leave from Air Force radio school before being shipped overseas. He was driving a 1956 Chevy Bel Air to his home in Los Angeles, when he came up on a less-than-courteous driver who crawled along the curves and sped up on the straights so that at first Mr. Bolomet couldn't pass him. But he finally did, and this is what happened:

"I had just started to get back to the rhythm of the road, when I saw the flashing red light of a New Mexico Highway Patrol car. Despite my pleas, we drove off

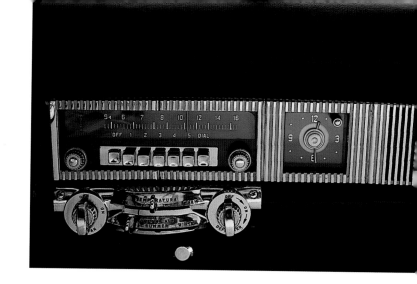

Opposite, above: 1958 Chevrolet Impala
Sport Coupe detail
Opposite, below: 1959 Dodge Custom Royal
Lancer Convertible detail
Right: 1952 Chrysler Imperial Newport detail

together to see the judge in his combination courthouse and curio store. After a steep and unpayable fine had been assessed, I was carted off to the Las Lunas County jail. By the time the sheriff reached my father, I had taught the local inmates the basics of 7 card stud, more or less learned how to roll Bull Durham, and learned to love a diet of soft-boiled eggs, Wonder bread, and hot, hot, hot peppers. When I finally got out, nearly a week later, the judge relented somewhat and gave me some really nice turquoise jewelry along with his best wishes."

—Yves Bolomet, Sylmar, California

Sputnik went up in 1957 and the jet age was launched. Aerospace had an immediate impact on automotive design—especially the designs of Raymond Loewy. What we really wanted to drive was our own personal rocket. Since rocketry was not available for sale to the ordinary public, kids in Southern California (many of them the sons of real-life rocket engineers working in the postwar aerospace industry) decided to build their own rockets and the hot-rod culture was born.

Even our commercial architecture was gravity defying: boomerangs, parabolas, and enormous sweeping awnings led us into the future, leading to a dismissal of history as outmoded. Modernism dominated our aesthetics. Neon-colored hula hoops and saddle shoes (resembling the latest new two-tone automotive paint schemes) became all the rage.

Postwar tract housing and the full-blown development of the commercial strip became reality. Enormous neon signs competed for the motorists' attention as they cruised that commercial strip. The opening of a new gas station was an occasion for a big promotion with beauty queens, clowns, and acrobats on hand to sign autographs. Taking a cue from the drive-in restaurant culture, some gas stations even put girls on roller skates attending cars.

Even though we still had a soft spot for what we now think of as programmatic architecture— those bigger-than-life eateries that beckoned the motorist (think of donut stands built in the form of giant donuts), times were changing. Much as we had become accustomed to the old walk-ups, where we placed our order at the counter, given our druthers we preferred not to leave our cars. And when we did, it was for the lure of air-conditioning. Proving that man could master the harsh environment, air-conditioning was an exemplary 1950s revolution. No single technological innovation did as much to kill drive-ins. Modern 1950s coffee shops flaunted their climate-controlled environment by integrating enormous plate glass windows with soaring rooflines. This new commercial architecture offered a brief respite from the heat and bustle of our car-crazed world outside.

Right: If you're into thrill rides, consider the 1957 Chevrolet Corvette as a worthy alternative to the "Giant Dipper" wooden roller coaster on the Santa Cruz, California, boardwalk.

1957 Chevrolet Corvette detail

1957 Chevrolet Bel Air Sport Coupe detail

With the two-lane blacktop stretching all the way to the horizon, this 1960 Chevrolet Corvette Convertible is the ultimate open-road car for the ultimate open-road highway—Route 66.

This new modern world may have looked inviting, but the future was not always up-to-date. Progress was slower for some than others:

"Being of Afro-American heritage, I recall specifically the lack of accommodations for lodging and dining for the (then) 'Colored.' Two outstanding incidents are etched in my memory—one in Flagstaff, Arizona, and another in a town in Texas. Realizing the discrimination of the day, I sought out a Mexican restaurant (off the route) in which to feed self and family in Flagstaff. Much to my surprise, we were refused service—and this was not the case in Los Angeles! [In a small town in Texas], I had grown weary from driving and sought out a Police Station for information on the location of a 'Colored' motel. If anyone had reliable information on a safe place to lodge overnight, the police certainly would be a good source, was my reasoning. The officer informed me 'there was none,' but made a kind offer of the use of an open cell! Of course, we declined the offer!"

—Ed Allen, Victorville, California

If air-conditioning was the death knell for the drive-in, the arrival of automotive air-conditioning was the birth of drive-thru. The McDonald's brothers recognized this when they modernized their operation to speed people in and out of the restaurant. Assembly-line efficiency served mealtime crowds quickly at the walk-up counter—why not apply the same principle to the drive-thru counter? It worked. McDonald's golden arches sprouted up across America. It was the beginning of the franchise—the seeds were sown for this popular business technique that would reach fruition later in the century.

Our franchised corporate culture has become a world standard in part due to the basic human fear of the unknown. When it comes to food, we like to know exactly how our hamburger will be prepared and at night we like to be guaranteed that our rooms will be clean. For some, though, the "lure of the lodge" was all part of traveling on the road:

"I remember that one of the highlights of each day's travel was the selection of a motel. In the '50s, most motels on Route 66 were still small, independently run operations of unknown quality. Selecting one was not a decision to be made lightly . . . . As my mother slowly drove along the main street, [we] three kids gave a running evaluation of the motels: 'swings and slides,' 'looks crummy,' 'that one has a restaurant.' 'Oohh! A swimming pool! Probably too expensive, but 'Can we Mom?'

"Narrowing our choices down to the top two or three, we made a second pass, stopping at each of the

Sunset is an appropriate setting for this 1951 Mercury Station Wagon, which is one of the last actual woody wagons—cars with real wood sides instead of the fake metal wood that characterized the early 1960s.

Like a refugee from a cartoon world, this 1959 Studebaker Lark motors down Route 66 on a prototypical Main Street in Stroud, Oklahoma. The Lark's clean, unassuming lines proved a big hit when it was introduced in 1959, tipping off automotive designers that the public had had enough of the chrome overkill and designer excesses that crept over American car makers in the late 1950s.

likely candidates. If the general consensus still prevailed after an external inspection, my mother would ask to see one of the rooms. In time, we got very good at this ritual, and rarely ended up in a place we didn't like.

"I'm sure it is because of those experiences that I tend to seek out state highways over interstates and small motels over the chain giants when I travel with my own family . . . .we still drive slowly down the main street while my kids call out an evaluation of each motel. ('Oohh, Dad. A swimming pool and cable!')"

—Chris Cavette, Fremont, California

As Einstein deconstructed the atom, roadside signs that gave our car culture direction pulsed with an "atomic" kinetic energy. Neon abounded. We were as seduced by these signs as we were by the jazz saxophone riffs of the day.

In Las Vegas, the 1950s saw the advent of the gargantuan sign. Las Vegas signs figuratively became the building, appropriating the individuality of the hotels they fronted in a concentrated image, allowing passersby (in cars) to judge their character at a glance. The Desert Inn and the Sands opened on the Strip with signs so big that nobody could miss them. The Las Vegas strip had a huge impact on roadside design worldwide, as depicted in architect Robert Venturi's pioneering book, *Learning from Las Vegas*.

Of course by the late 1950s popular culture became a target for elite critics who called it "trash." The good taste mavens were even massacring our cars. Under this critical fire, Detroit backed off from the fin mania, which peaked by the late 50s. The 1960 Cadillac sedan fin design was noticeably scaled back from the previous years. Cars reversed direction and began to shrink in scale, concentrating on the impression of greater efficiency in the service of space-age speed.

That's not all that shrank. The early 1960s marked a pullback in commercial architecture design as well. Spare cinder block gas stations replaced the porcelain enamel palaces of the past. We were entering another less-is-more era and roadside America's carnival-like atmosphere began to pale.

Opposite: Life certainly would be "nice" behind the wheel of this 1961 Buick Invicta either with or without the Coca-Cola.

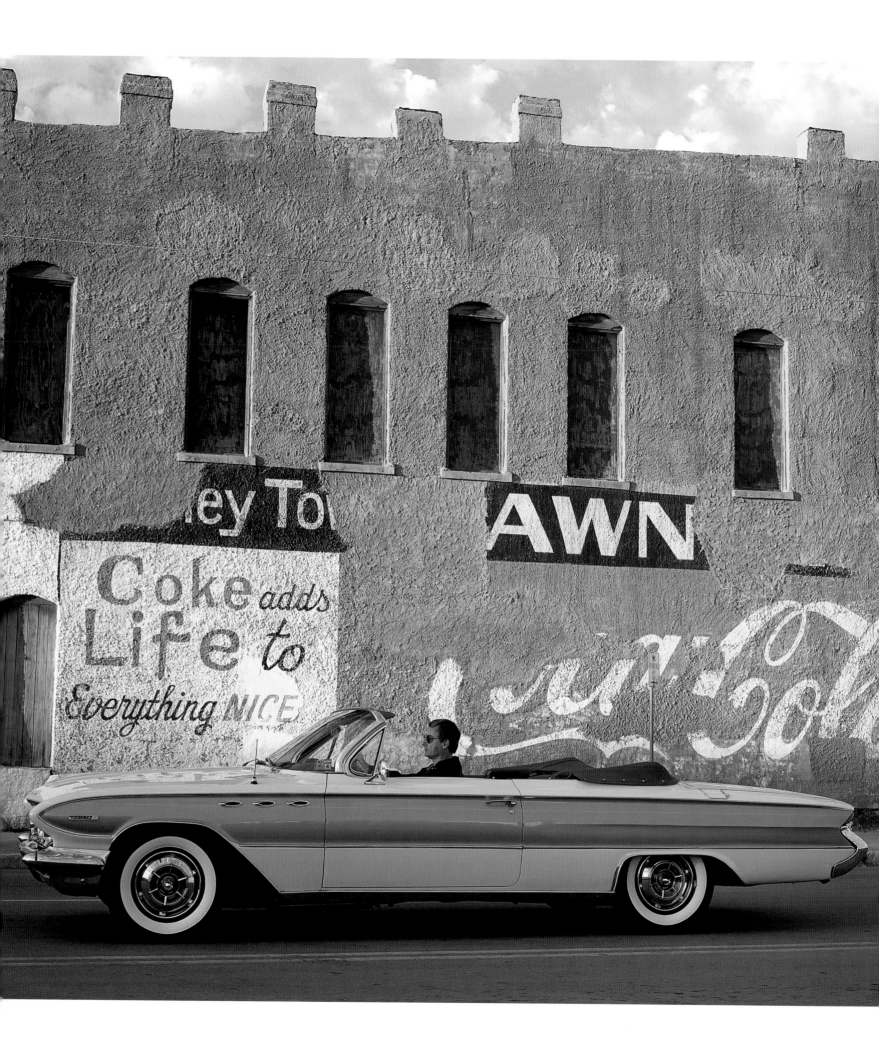

Left: The untouched landscape of the Laguna Indian Reservation stretches through miles of New Mexico desert, traversed by the Rio Puerco river. Equally pristine are the lines of this pale blue 1957 Thunderbird Convertible. Predating the modern comforts of the 1950s (dubbed "the era of excess and accessories"), the Thunderbird recalls a leaner approach to motoring.

Overleaf: If manna is from heaven, what is the origin of this white 1959 Oldsmobile Super 88 Holiday Scenic Coupe? Detroit cooked up a masterwork with this land yacht, a term that's no exaggeration because it's a full 9 inches wider and 10 inches longer than any previous model. Heck, it's even bigger than the White Manna! The Art Deco-inspired White Manna Hamburger diner was actually built for the 1939 World's Fair to give visitors a futuristic look at fast food. Manna burgers are quite small—about the size of a flattened golf ball. This Olds could eat more than a few!

The vivid image of the El Vado Indian chief looms above this 1958 Ford Fairlane Skyliner Retractable Convertible Coupe like a neon sunset. Machinery necessary to convert from hardtop to let-it-all-hang-out convertible? Seven reversible electric motors, 10 power relays, and 12 limit switches.

Left: The comet in the sky above this 1956 Ford Fairlane Victoria is the rare period neon sign at the Comet Lanes in Grand Rapids, Michigan. The sign memorializes the glory of bowling's finest hour with chase lights (bulbs that flash on and off in sequence), which mimic the path of the bowling ball hitting the pins. With cross-generational and multi-ethnic appeal, bowling was the suburban 1950s sport: it brought social cohesiveness and fun to the melting pot that was suburban life in America at the time.

Opposite: Rarely have things been cozier at the Cozy Drive-In in Netcong, New Jersey, than with this fleet of vintage lovelies tucked in side-by-side. Something about the rounded lines of these 1950s favorites suggests comfort food—a frothy milk shake, a spattering hot burger, or a big basket of crispy fries with ketchup. These cars are all Chevrolets (models include the Bel Air, Corvette, Impala, Biscayne, and Malibu) with the exception of a Ford Crown Victoria and a Buick Riviera; they date between 1955 and 1964, providing an indelible record of automotive styling during those years.

Ted Drewes has provided an Arctic refuge for overheated residents of St. Louis, Missouri, since 1929. The family's private custard recipes inspire fervor in its fans: local police have sometimes been called out to keep traffic flowing as steaming citizens line up for their cool fuel. Almost hot enough to thaw the icicles off Ted Drewes is this spectacular 1953 Buick Skylark. Built to celebrate Buick's 50th anniversary, this limited-production cherry chariot is not for the fainthearted. It features Buick's first V-8 engine and a chopped windshield, which, together with the sensationally dipped beltline, make it the automotive embodiment of a fireworks display. With a hot ride like this Buick, a cool custard stop is a necessity.

Below: Though built after the heyday of the Mother Road, the Route 66 Diner in Albuquerque, New Mexico, commemorates the days when the town was an oasis for travelers making the long desert trek. The Diner's top-notch Blue Plate Special and other menu delights make it a worthy successor to Sam's classic 66 Service Station, which used to occupy its place. One of the cars Sam would have serviced is this 1957 Ford Thunderbird, Ford's answer to the European sports cars GI's fell for while serving abroad. This model includes a radio whose volume changes with the car's speed to compensate for wind noise—a musical version of cruise control. Raymond Loewy's design for the 1960 Studebaker Hawk takes the Thunderbird's lines into the jet age. Aircraft styling influenced Loewy's jaunty tail fins, reflecting America's passion for rocket-inspired design.

Opposite: This 1955 Chevrolet Bel Air top-of-the-line convertible was a high-class ride that featured Chevrolet's first V-8 engine. There's a suggestion of a jet-age aesthetic, but the car retains an organic friendliness, with its visored headlights giving it an almost animal demeanor. One of the friendliest restaurants ever is Bob's Big Boy, a fast-food franchise whose mascot is the smiling big boy with a huge burger held aloft. This branch is the oldest surviving example of the chain. Designed in 1949 by architect Wayne McAllister, it epitomizes postwar "Coffee Shop Moderne" architecture and was recently declared a historic landmark in its hometown of Burbank, California.

Above: The Boots Motel in Carthage, Missouri, is a classic from the early days of motor tourism. At its 1939 opening, the Boots advertised "A Radio in Every Room" (these days, discerning readers will notice "HBO" spelled out in Gothic letters). The covered carport with every room is a reminder of when cars were considered a coveted luxury rather than the necessity they have become. By the time this 1955 DeSoto Firedome Sportsman came along, cars were the predominant form of travel in America. Novelty became key to car design and sales. This DeSoto was part of a much-ballyhooed "Forward Look" styling campaign. It features DeSoto's first tail fins and an arresting steel-framed wraparound windshield with optional Sun-cap visor.

Left: A trio of fabulous Thunderbirds clusters in the parking lot of their namesake motel in Joplin, Missouri, like guests of honor. From left to right are the 1955, 1958, and 1957 models of the famed Ford Thunderbird.

Fifties pastel colors and the 1956 Ford Thunderbird.

One of the coolest examples of Streamline Moderne architecture was the Coral Court Motel of St. Louis, Missouri, on Route 66. The Court featured a truly modern innovation: garages adjoined each room via an inner door, allowing visitors to enter and exit without scrutiny from the prying eyes of the outside world. Ironically, this innovation made the Coral Court notorious as one of the original "no-tell" motels. After many a steamy night, alas, the Coral Court has been torn down. Every bit as sleek but a good deal more public are the snappy lines of this unforgettable 1957 Chrysler 300 2-door hardtop. Designer Virgil Exner sounded a battle cry: "Longer, Lower, Sleeker, Wider." This zesty sedan, with its wolflike tail fins, is one of his most spectacular accomplishments.

Rosie's Diner in Rockford, Michigan, on Highway M-57 is renowned for its great food, homemade pies, and glorious neon—"Good food served right." Manufactured by the Paramount Dining Company in 1945, Rosie's was featured in numerous Bounty Paper Towel commercials where Rosie the waitress swiped counters and declared Bounty to be the "quicker-picker upper" for rapt TV audiences. Patrons of the home cookin' are the occupants of the 1960 Chevrolet Corvette, 1956 Ford Fairlane Victoria, 1953 Oldsmobile Rocket 98, 1960 Cadillac Sedan DeVille, and 1960 Ford Thunderbird.

Overleaf: Surrounded by a swarm of finned beauties from the 1950s and 60s, the Elgin Diner is the place to eat in Camden, New Jersey. The silver 1961 Plymouth Suburban Wagon is a particularly amazing specimen. Built at a time when Chrysler design stylist Virgil Exner was mandating "the Forward Look," this car features bizarre "twin pod" instrumentation panels and a square Lucite steering wheel! Purchased by its current owners in 1961, the Elgin still serves the best of food with the best of service to all drivers, car vintage notwithstanding.

Opposite: Geography purists might carp that Coney Island is far removed from this restaurant in the land-locked Massachusetts city of Worcester. But hey, is every Paris cleaners in Paris? The hot dogs at Worcester's Coney Island are famous—originally cut from a spool by its jolly proprietor—and are every bit as juicy as their New York progenitors. Under the enormous enamel and neon sign is another classic: the 1957 Chevrolet Bel Air.

Here at Angelo's Hamburgers—a family operation in California's Central Valley—it's all in a day's work to pull the top out of the hat, as it were. The red-and-white color scheme of this 1958 Ford Skyliner Retractable Fairlane 500 accentuates the mechanical drama of a hardtop lowering into the trunk with push-button ease.

S C I M I T A R

1957 Scimitar All-Purpose Sedan detail

Located at the Texan "Crossroads of America" (where Route 66 crosses Mexico-to-Canada Route 83), the U-Drop-Inn was built in 1936 as a meeting-place for local ranchers: it got its name from a contest won by an 8-year-old boy. The 1956 Chevrolet Bel Air and 1955 Ford Fairlane Sedans are right at home. With solid construction and pleasing pastel paint jobs, these sedans are the kind of upstanding workhorses that ferried Texas citizens across its plains at the time the classic *Giant* hit the screen.

Like thoroughbreds at a trough, these stunning finned 50s mobiles line up at famed Mearle's College Drive-In of Visalia, California. In the 1940s and 50s, Mearle's was a renowned destination for those seeking to beat the Central California heat. Carhop service allowed sweltering patrons to enjoy ice cream or soda without having to leave the car. The 1963 advent of air-conditioning changed the habits of Mearle's patrons, who then preferred indoor dining. Curbside service remains an option since Mearle's is faithful to its history: its original building is still intact.

DINER

Al Mac

JUSTLY FAMOUS SINCE 19[..]

Les Desserts

Massachusetts
R 9487 A
REPAIR

KENNEDY
JOHNSON '60

The parking lot of Al Mac's restaurant in Fall River, Massachusetts, is a riot of color and geometry—a buffet of colorful and tasty vintage delights. From left to right they are: 1957 Oldsmobile Super 88 Holiday Coupe, 1957 Chevrolet Bel Air Sport Coupe, 1958 Chevrolet Corvette Convertible, 1955 Chevrolet Bel Air 4-Door Sedan, and 1964 Ford Galaxie 500 Convertible.

Below: Ever since the owners of this once-humble trading post struck piping hot mineral water (112 degrees) while sinking a well in 1939, the Buckhorn Baths in Mesa, Arizona, has been a mecca for privileged types intent on benefitting from the healthful waters. What luminaries might have driven these three phenomenal vehicles to the Buckhorn? It's hard not to think of Marilyn Monroe when noticing the outrageous tail fins of the 1959 Cadillac Coupe DeVille. The 1940 Packard 110 Convertible Coupe is an example of an upscale brand that successfully adapted itself to middle-class audiences—Lana Turner, perhaps, or maybe Betty Grable? The elegant 1931 LaSalle Model 345A Convertible Coupe won plaudits for designer Harley Earl, who was inspired by the lines of the famous Hispano-Suiza.

Right: Built in 1931 and operated as a taxidermy, trading post, and tourist attraction, America's largest log cabin was converted into a saloon in 1936 by one Doc Williams. In the 1960s and 70s, the Museum Club's prime Route 66 location made it a venue for country music's rising and established stars, including Willie Nelson and Waylon Jennings. Like a medley of poignant and racy country tunes, immaculate vintage cars from the Route 66 Car Club cram the Museum Club's lot.

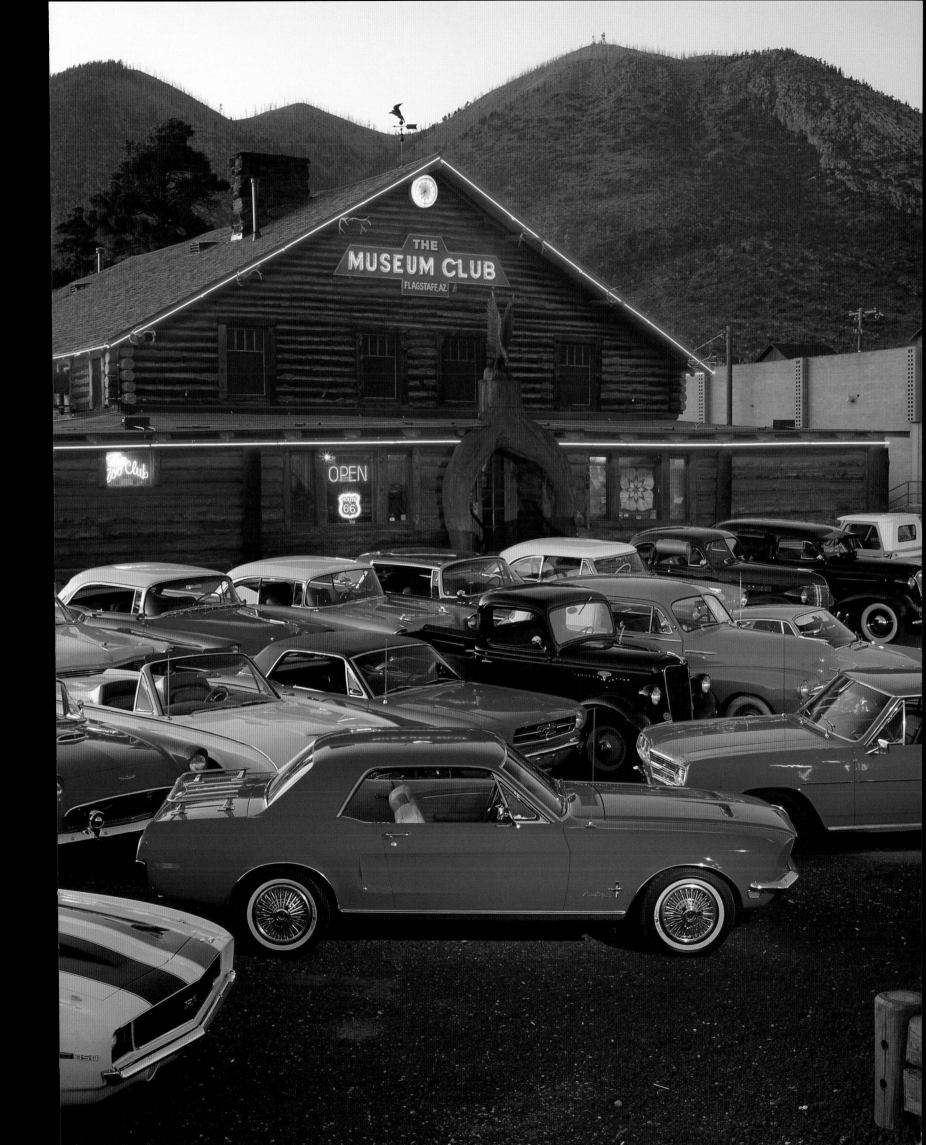

Raymond Loewy's 1953 Studebaker Starliner embodied continental subtlety just as America was peaking in its postwar enthusiasm for automotive behemoths. With its wraparound rear window and clean lines, the Starliner was the first American car to be exhibited in the Museum of Modern Art, New York. Although Loewy's spare design was out of step with the 50s market, his foresight stood out when the 1960s automotive designs picked up on his minimalist cues. Completed in 1961, the LAX theme building was a crystallization of the unbridled dreams and optimism at the dawn of the Jet Age. The promise of a better tomorrow was embodied in the building's design by a team of architects led by William Pereira.

This modest, all American hot-dog stand is the setting for a 1957 Chrysler 300C convertible that represents the best of late 1950s styling. The elegantly swooped fins and tastefully modeled grill make the car a model of restraint in an era of overkill.

This yellow 1956 Ford Thunderbird Convertible stands in front of the Tower Theater, a recently refurbished example of a classic 1940s movie palace.

Below: The El Monte drive-in recalls the heyday of
drive-in movies, when they were as much a car
show as a movie-going experience. Cars such as
this 1954 Chevrolet Bel Air Coupe provided status as well as privacy for more intimate
moments inspired by the romance of the movies.

Right: It's easy to imagine Audrey Hepburn as
Sabrina looking wistfully out of the carriage
house window at this 1953 Packard Caribbean
Convertible, which could well have been driven
by William Holden in Billy Wilder's film Sabrina.

Left: This 1957 Lincoln Premier 4-Door Sedan design was typical of the exuberant decoration found on American cars in the finned era. Equally buoyant is the Uniroyal Tire, a fitting tribute to the Motor City. The 80-foot tire began life as a ferris wheel—it was Uniroyal's entry in the 1964 New York World's Fair. After the fair, the gondolas were replaced by simulated tread and the tire was relocated outside Detroit's Interstate 94, where it has become a famous landmark.

Above: This blood-encrusted Tyrannosaurus (looking a little like a sentry from a 1950s Japanese horror flick) has given a thrill to generations of visitors at the Grand Canyon caverns. Real Tyrannosaurs (after a few millennia beneath the sod) provided fossil fuel for this 1953 Cadillac Series 62 Coupe. Designer Bill Mitchell modified the 1948 model with the toothy "Dagmar" front bumper not unlike the grin of T-Rex behind.

With road signs as big as a billboard, who needs maps? That was the marketing plan of Meramec Caverns promoter Les Dill, who paid for barn-side advertising on all roads in the vicinity. Also employed in the advertising scheme were grade-school kids who got paid to post visiting cars (like this 1954 Chevrolet Bel Air) with bumper stickers advertising the underground caverns, which are touted as a one-time hideout of Jesse James.

Left: This Nash Ambassador is an intrepid guest on gleaming Fremont Street in Las Vegas. Built for a generation of salesmen, the Ambassador features a back seat that folds down to provide a sleeping area for those so full of entrepreneurial spirit and thrift that they can't bear laying out money for a motel.

Above: One of the few Asian restaurants along Route 66, the Grand Canyon Café has been owned and operated by the same family since its founding in 1938. Its specialty, American Chop Suey, has galvanized many a traveler to press on for the nearby Grand Canyon. Barely pausing for a refuel, this 1955 Lincoln Capri is a speedster in luxury duds. By the 1950s, Lincoln moved away from its country club origins to the thrills of open-road racing. Lincoln dominated the legendary Carrera Panamericana road races between 1952–54, but suffered from staid styling left over from its white-shoe days. The button-down duckling became a speed swan with the restyled Lincoln Capri, whose tighter lines reflected its road-racing capabilities and left the polo-and-tennis crowd eating dust.

In pre–air-conditioning days, drivers sweltering through the Arizona deserts dreamed of staying cool. Motels like the Starlite erected neon artwork to exploit those fantasies, aiming to bring even the most callous speed demon to a grinding halt. Like a Siren to the sweaty traveler, the bathing-suited lady beckons us to follow her into an endlessly repeating cascade of neon.

1957 Packard Clipper Country Sedan detail

This "fintastic" portrait depicts what can only be described as a duel. On the left, the 1959 Cadillac Sedan DeVille. On the right, the 1959 Cadillac Fleetwood 60 Special. To the victor go the spoils, and may the longest tail win.

Above: Clearly the envy of its 1950s counterpart across the way, this white 1962 Chevrolet Impala Super Sport Convertible serenely enjoys its status as the happenin' ride at the Dog 'n Suds. Increasing horsepower became a marketing angle in the early 60s, and the Impala offered one of the highest performance engines in Chevy history (409 cu, 425 bhp). Low and wide were the operative design words for this period in mercurial Detroit, with the chrome-laden bulk of the 50s a distant memory.

Left: We've all heard that things are bigger in Texas, but the hood ornament on this 1960 Cadillac Series 62 Convertible gives new meaning to the phrase. These longhorns add a rakish touch to the otherwise restrained Caddy, with its especially large wraparound windshield. Equally outrageous is the challenge at the Big Texan Steak Ranch, which restores drama to the high plains by offering a free 72-ounce (that's 4 lb.) steak to anybody who can finish it in an hour at one sitting.

Opposite: Deep in Philadelphia lies the birthplace of the world-famous Philly cheese steak or "hoagie." At Ground Zero stands Geno's, a key purveyor of the best examples of the genre. This 1959 Chevrolet Impala was significantly larger than preceding models, in keeping with concurrent public taste for "bigger is better." The Impala is distinguished by its "batmobile" fins: reviewers have commented that the rear deck is "big enough to land a Piper Cub."

Like a hungry hound, this 1961 Imperial Crown Convertible seems to crouch outside this neat little café hoping for a morsel to be tossed from the kitchen. Faced with constant competition from the better-known Cadillacs and Lincolns of the world, the luxury Imperial struggled to stake out its own stylistic identity. Imperial succeeded with this 1961 model, which featured many radical stylistic devices such as classic headlights—chrome bullets nestled in scooped-out fenders—and "gunsight" tail lamps encircled by freestanding chrome bands. With its insouciant fins and jazzy front grille (notice the hep-cat off-center insignia) this convertible was truly a bachelor's companion of the highest order.

Swanky and oversized, this 1960 Lincoln Mark V Convertible is the ideal car to impress the sharkskin suits at Trader Vic's, one of Hollywood's best-known and beloved nightspots.

ROADSIDE AMERICA

Above: One of only two surviving examples of a
Sterling Streamliner diner (and the first diner ever to
be registered as a National Historic Place), the
Modern Diner in Pawtucket, Rhode Island, catches
the eye of highway drivers with its bullet-like design.
The clean lines of the enamel-clad exterior create a
brisk, in-and-out feeling, reassuring travelers that
they won't wait long for service. Equally streamlined,
the debonair Studebaker Commander Starlight
Coupe seems to be moving even at rest. The famous
"bullet-nose" front end was designer Raymond
Loewy's conscious salute to the airplane, and the
spectacular three-element rear window further
contributes to its streamlined appearance.

Left: As the 1960s began, Cadillac designers began
streamlining the 1950s curves. While this 1960
Cadillac Sedan DeVille still has fins, they come as
afterthoughts to the tapering rear that recalls a
turbine shape. An oversized windshield and delicate
roof struts augment the lighter-than-air feeling of
this very large vehicle.

The vibrant Metro Diner is a neon mecca in downtown Tulsa, Oklahoma. The Metro draws loyal customers from far and wide with its famous meringue pies and 50s faves like chicken pot pie and meatloaf. Looking a little like desserts, these Nash Metropolitans are almost cute enough to eat. Produced by the American Motor Corporation between 1954 and 1962, the Nashes have a distinctly low-cal yet very sweet feeling: remember cyclamates? With a tiny body powered by a 1500 ci, 4-cylinder engine designed specifically for "neighborhood driving," the Nash was ahead of its time in anticipating the 1970s trend toward fuel economy. Left to right, these models hail from 1957, 1959, 1960, 1961, and 1962

The triumvirate of road power parked at the Bendix Diner in Hasbrouk, New Jersey, runs the historical gamut, from a 1950s classic to the road-burning early 1970s. From left to right are the 1971 Plymouth Valiant Duster 340 Coupe, 1950 Ford Convertible, and 1967 Pontiac Grand Prix.

At the Degadillo Snow Cap café in Seligman, Arizona, this customized 1923 Model T Roadster flashes past its more domesticated brethren, the 1955 Chevrolet Bel Air, the 1967 Pontiac GTO Convertible, the 1957 Chevrolet Bel Air, and the 1966 Ford Mustang Convertible. The innovative Snow Cap signage leads us to wonder what kind of patrons induced the "no . . . feet on walls" prohibition. Interior signs are deadpan too: "Dead Chicken Sandwiches," "Cheeseburgers with Cheese," and "Male and Female Sandwiches."

Left: The eccentric Space Age Lodge in Gila Bend, Arizona, and this super-cool 1960 Cadillac Fleetwood Model 60 Special 4-Door Sedan are both obsessed with the same phenomenon—the mystical lure of outer space and America's obsession to get there.

Above: Glowing taillights in the mile-wide fins of the 1960 Cadillac Fleetwood Model 60 Special 4-Door Sedan create an otherworldly feeling, as if the car might be an alien vehicle.

Woodies, Encinitas, California

Car lot with lightbulbs, Visalia, California

Above: Joe & Aggies Café, Arizona
Overleaf: On Route 66, Arizona

In a classic case of perception versus reality, the gentlemen here look like they're in trouble. Their immaculate 1956 Ford Fairlane Club Sedan has broken down in what appears to be rattlesnake country. The reality: this theatrical sign near McLean, Texas, is no guarantee of rattlers nearby. Dating from the early 1950s, this advertisement to Route 66 drivers contributed to the expression *tourist trap*. Townspeople used to lay dead snakes across the road to discourage visitors: the site closed in the mid 60s. The stalwart Fairlane is good protection nonetheless: it originated many safety features, including seat belts (a hit that outstripped Ford's supply), breakaway rearviews, and crash-proof door locks.

Busted, Arizona

Above: Chrysler, Fancy Town, North Carolina
Opposite: Hairpin curves, Oatman, Arizona
Overleaf: Roy's Café, Motel, and Gas east of Barstow, California

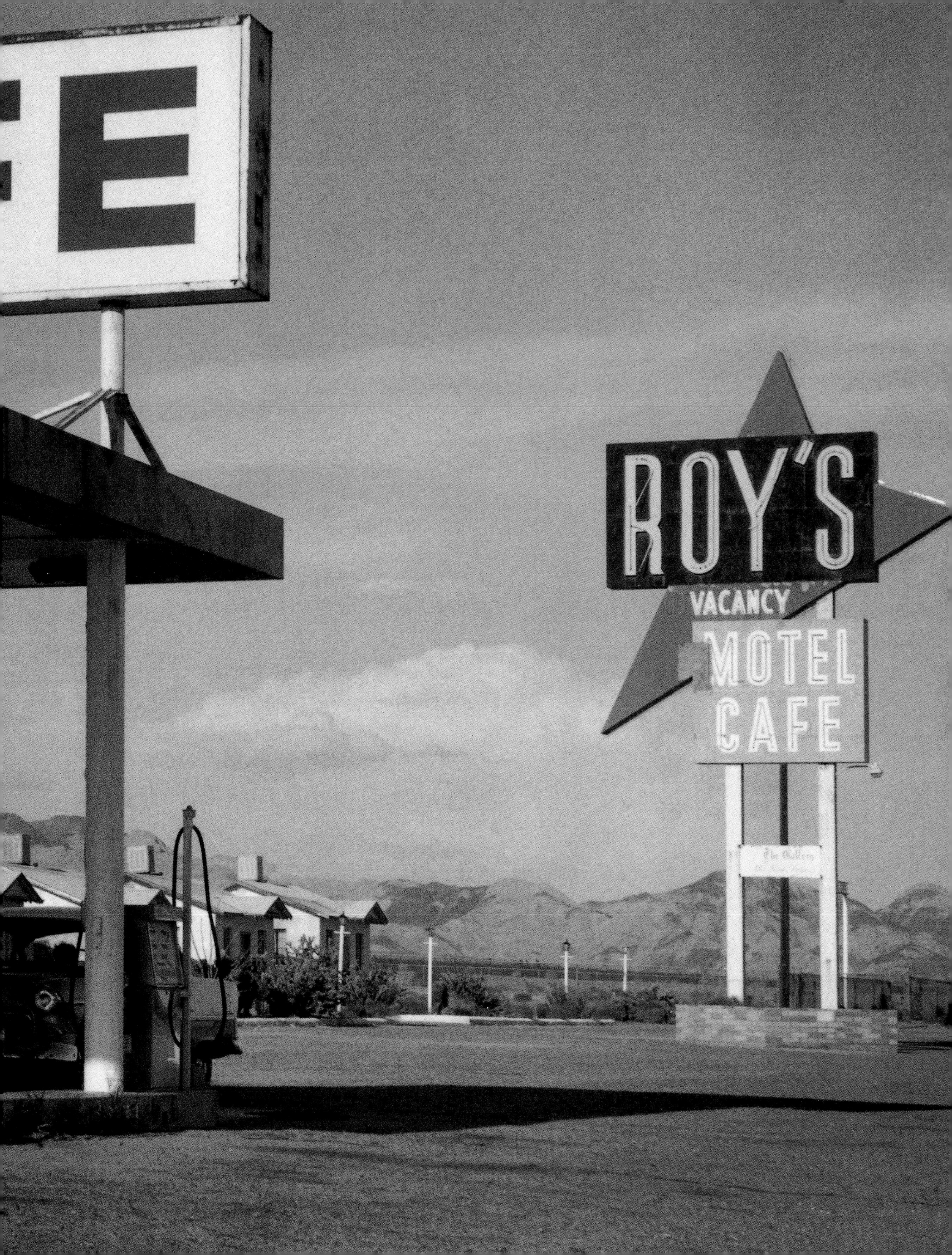
ROY'S
VACANCY
MOTEL
CAFE

Breakdown, Mojave Desert, Arizona

Opposite: Any cross-country trip worth its salt includes a stop for mechanical contemplation. The music of racheting jack and passing cars merges with the hum of roadside crickets as we pause for adjustments. This "breakdown" is no comment on the Rambler—they were great cars with thrifty 6-cylinder engines and clever space utilization, a tradition soon after abandoned by Detroit and carried on by the Japanese. Perhaps this immaculate 1961 Rambler Cross Country Classic has succumbed to the lure of the jackrabbits on this stretch of road near Joseph City, Arizona. Founded by a marketing whiz who saw that Burma Shave had hit on a great idea, the Jack Rabbit Trading Post erected a long string of cryptic billboards featuring the jackrabbit against a yellow background. After miles of these images, drivers were dying of curiosity, so the "here it is" billboard was a welcome notice that their questions were about to be answered.

End of the road, Santa Rosa, New Mexico

Right: More than just a meal in itself, this 1955 Cadillac Fleetwood 8-Passenger Sedan is a lavish feast for everybody in the vicinity. With enough room for the whole family, the Fleetwood 8 could fit grandparents and even a few step-relatives. Part of a limited production run, this car was mostly used as a limousine. It's similar to the formal Fleetwood Limousine Morgan Freeman used to chauffeur Jessica Tandy in the movie Driving Miss Daisy. Long famous for its hot dogs smothered in french fries and "sport" peppers (that's hot, to the uninitiated), Henry's has been satisfying Route 66 customers since 1950.

Opposite: Tail fins, El Reno, Oklahoma

Left: Thunderbird dashboard, Laguna, New Mexico

Below: By the side of the endless two-lane blacktop, this formidable yet curvaceous 1957 Chevrolet Cameo pickup truck is a memorable marker. Trucks like this were a bulwark against the cruel forces of the desert.

Above: Tower service station, Shamrock, Texas

Right: In 1949 the American Dream was gradually rising from the ashes of World War II, with its memories of shortage and hardship. This 1949 Ford Deluxe Business Coupe reflects a dream that's still hesitant. With its low window-space to body-mass ratio, the Ford seems designed to protect passengers more than later designs, which had the confidence to open up the proportion of window space and create panoramic visibility. Hinting at prosperity, this model was specifically tailored to salesmen, with the back seat omitted to allow for their sample cases as they traveled from city to city. The rich ox blood color and robust form of this give it a visual if not a thematic fellowship with the bovine mascot of the unforgettable beef burger restaurant in Amarillo, Texas.

6.
MUSCLE CARS FOR THE SPACE AGE
1964-1970

AFTER DECADES OF PLANNING AND CONSTRUCTION, the long-dreamed-of interstate highway system became reality. Unfortunately, the new highways circumnavigated most of the colorful (albeit jumbled) mom-and-pop commercial strips that had grown around America's early roadside routes. Major sections of Route 66—our first highway love—were bypassed and forgotten after the interstates were christened. The absence of traffic caused many once vibrant establishments to close their doors.

The interstates proved to be a mixed blessing for the motorist. On the one hand, traffic flow improved, significantly reducing journey times. But our trips were no longer quite as

Preceding pages: The initiator of the "Pony Car Revolution," this 1964 half Ford Mustang is one of the most influential automotive designs Detroit ever produced. The immediate popularity of the pony cars bolstered Detroit's confidence in producing a line of increasingly faster vehicles later dubbed "Muscle Cars." Also representing the best of an era is Billy's Service Station, formerly of Anaheim, California. Sadly, Billy's, one of the rare stations where you could actually get service, has fallen victim to the wrecking ball. Sole proprietorships like Billy's fight an uphill battle in an increasingly franchise-driven world.

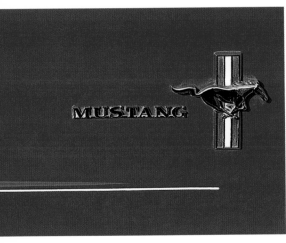

Ford Mustang badge

much fun. Adventures along the roadside became limited to obtaining the necessities—gas and food—at the fastest possible speed. With no commercial strip to distract us along the new roads, we began to concentrate on horsepower. Terry Sullivan recalls his 1964 trip across Route 66 as:

"... two lanes of weirdness. I was in a borrowed 1963 Buick wagon full of 200-pound football players, heading to California from Michigan for the Rose Bowl. Going uphill, the top speed we could muster was 30 MPH. Downhill we could make 100 MPH. For three states we continually passed one guy downhill and he passed us going uphill."

—Terry Sullivan, Monterey, California

Our need for speed was great. Chrysler's Hemi engine of the 1950s had kicked off the horsepower race and the 1960s saw its culmination. American auto manufacturers began to feel the influence of European road-racing design. The exploits of a new breed of American hero—the race car driver—fueled our lust for speed. Major American racers of the day—Phil Hill, Carroll Shelby, and Richard Petty—became household names.

Speed was important to the summertime motorist because of the breeze it generated through opened windows. To stop moving, or even to slow down, was to risk suffocation in the heat. Air-conditioning was still a pricey feature for most Americans: the early 1960s economic downturn positioned air-conditioning as a clear luxury option. Consequently, most families sweltered through car trips on summer vacations:

"In 1964, I loaded my wife and our two kids, ages 4 and 2, into our un-air-conditioned Plymouth Valiant for a journey from Washington, D.C. to Barstow, CA . . . . As in pioneer days, I tried to drive 400 miles before stopping . . . 4 of us, 2 kids under 4, in an unair-conditioned car on Route 66 in July. I felt like the wagonmaster trying to keep the renegade troops on the trail . . . . It seemed as though we were on the trail for 4 months, but [it] was really 4 days . . . . We took the route that led across the cool Rockies through Denver back home. If we had tried Route 66, I would have been divorced and my kids would never have forgiven me to this day."

—The Rev. Barron Maberry, Washington, D.C.

If Detroit couldn't offer us affordable air-conditioning for our cars, American ingenuity found a way to cool the passengers:

"As a kid, I always looked forward to our family treks from San Diego to Michigan for family reunions . . . . One particularly memorable trip took us from San Bernardino to Chicago through some of the hottest and driest country I've ever seen before or since. I don't remember the summer of 1964 being significantly hotter than any other year, but with all seven of us packed in that 1963 Rambler Classic 660 station wagon, the heat became unbearable. On the outskirts of Oklahoma City, we found our salvation . . . a $5 air conditioner! It consisted of an ingeniously folded cardboard box that hung through the partially opened front passenger's window. The box was filled to the brim with dry ice. As the car picked up speed, outside air was forced through the opening in the front of the box across and through the dry ice . . . . We were in heaven!"

—William I. Waite, Oak Harbor, Washington

During this period, the Big Three automakers marketed two different product lines. On the one hand, they tried to sell the consumer on compact, more economical cars, but on the other hand their fascination with horsepower grew unabated. Even the mass-marketed "Pony Cars" that trotted onto the scene had names evocative of speed like Mustang and Firebird. A new low-slung design aesthetic shucked fifties chrome doodads in favor of lean styling and faster performance.

Detroit butted heads with Washington. Car safety, led by Ralph Nader, became a widespread issue. The idea that a cherished and beloved little car could injure you through no fault of your own was a new one for Americans: taking responsibility for public safety was an issue not easily embraced by auto manufacturers. Seat belts and air bags became hotly contested features. Topping it all off, First Lady Ladybird Johnson went on the warpath with her "Beautify America" campaign. Unfortunately much of roadside America became her target.

Road signs along the interstates exemplified a new way of life. As the signs grew bigger, the buildings they advertised became less interesting. Bold signage allowed burgeoning fast food, motel, and gasoline franchises to economize on their structures in order not to distract from the corporate logo featured on the signs. Golden arches began to disappear from McDonald's restaurant structures, for example, only to crop up in more standardized format on their signage. Bigger signage dovetailed with the need for speed—cars traveling at 60 to 70 MPH needed super-visible signs in order to slow down without causing an accident.

Opposite: Many movie palaces have gone the way of drive-ins and other roadside dinosaurs, but the Wilson Theater survives intact, as does this 1968 Chevrolet Z28 Camaro.

Below: The expansive hood on this 1970 Plymouth Barracuda is interrupted by an enormous hood scoop designed to gulp air for the lightning quick Hemi engine.

Like everything else, gas stations became simpler and more economical. Where gas stations and diners once stood as imposing architectural monuments, buildings of the 1960s were more likely built of cinder block. Plastic—the miracle building material of the 50s—was used to mimic the more expensive neon lighting effects of the past.

With the race to space won, we began to pull back from the future. Gone were the wide glass expanses and soaring rooflines designers used to attract attention along our roadsides in the honeymoon of the early 1950s. Instead we looked back to the past, with its low rooflines and natural materials. In suburbia, commercial architecture evolved to blend in with the tract housing surrounding it. Low-roof, ranch-style structures became more popular. Canopies reappeared to shelter our still-hallowed automobiles.

During the 1960s, we may have pulled back from the future in our roadside architecture designs, but horsepower still ruled our hearts. Cars ran faster and faster across the land.

Right: What could be more patriotic than a gigantic flag and this true-blue 1967 Chevrolet Corvette Stingray Convertible? Hail to the chief of high performance, Detroit-style.

1964 half Ford Mustang steering wheel

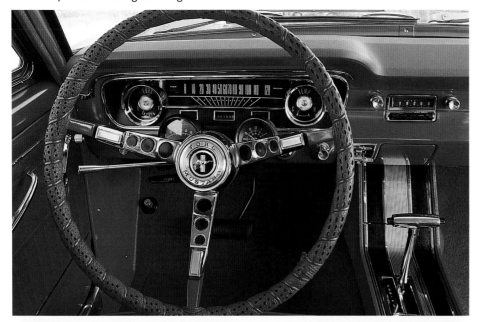

1968 half Ford Mustang Cobra Jet detail

This 1965 Mercer Cobra is a design exercise by Virgil Exner to show the many uses of copper and its alloys as automotive brightwork.

Stations like KNGS in California's Central Valley have always been a home for subversive, road-burnin' tunes like the ones that fueled this 1970 Plymouth Hemi Roadrunner through many a flamin' drag race.

Looking every inch like a hornet in flight, this yellow-and-black 1970 Oldsmobile Cutlass 442 W-30 hovers near Madame Sophia the palm reader.

Nothing says "Southern California" quite as loud as a soft-top and this sky blue 1964 Ford Thunderbird Convertible. With a tail fin tapering to brake lights that look like a jet's afterburners glow, this T-Bird is a valentine to the sky-cowboys of the time. Advertising referred to the "Thunderbird Cockpit" and its "flight deck," which included a battery of warning lights for malfunctions. Another California contribution to pop culture is the "Tail of the Pup" restaurant, whose programmatic architecture informs us instantly as to its purpose. Its curvaceous bun and protruding dog conjure up a multitude of associations. Built in 1946, the Pup remains a beloved fixture in its Los Angeles neighborhood and in numerous films, where its appearance instantly signifies Lotus Land.

Left: The 1964 Pontiac GTO Convertible became a legend the minute it hit the streets. A closely guarded secret for a year before its introduction, the GTO was the brainchild of GM's John DeLorean and Jim Wangers. The moment this baby's dual exhaust pipes rattled windows, the secret was out: its optional 389 cubic-inch V-8 tripower engine launches it from 0–60 MPH in 4.6 seconds. Every bit as assertive as the GTO is this towering Donut—a landmark on the L.A. skyline that's built 30 feet high to attract Angelenos from the nearby 405 free-way. Once called the BIG DONUT (how'd they come up with that one?), Randy's Donuts is now known as the "Mecca of dunkin'" and claims to be the world's first fast food drive-in.

Above: Designed to replace the Corvair and compete with the new Mustang, the 1968 Chevrolet Camaro SS 396 surged ahead with an identity all its own. Equally unique are the burgers served at White Castle. The unusual square, smaller-than-a-full-meal burgers are affectionately known as "sliders," "belly-bombers," "gut-busters" and our favorite—"beef cookies."

Opposite: This 1966 Shelby GT350 materializes like a ghost against the darkening sky above the Santa Monica pier. Located at the Western terminus of Route 66, the Santa Monica Pier projects into the Pacific Ocean like "The End" at the conclusion of a great novel.

1970 Plymouth Superbird

Overleaf: Hollywood came calling when scouts chose The Big 8 Motel for Tom Cruise and Dustin Hoffman to play a crucial scene in 1988's Rain Man. *The motel's actual location in El Reno, Oklahoma, didn't suit the story, necessitating the "Amarillo's Finest" sign, which proprietors have kept as a souvenir. Just as aggressive as the Big 8's signage is this 1968 Plymouth Road Runner, which was described as "the most brazenly pure and non-compromising super car in history" by* Motor Trend *magazine. Aimed at the "eat a burger, burn some rubber" crowd, the Road Runner was designed to accelerate to 100 MPH within a quarter mile.*

Below: The enormous porcelain enamel and neon sign of the Westerner Motel is too much to resist for this 1968 Cadillac DeVille Convertible.

Left: If the hustle and bustle of modern life gets to be too much, consider some time-travel courtesy of Las Vegas's Luxor hotel. Located just a block from the "Statue of Liberty" on the famed Vegas Strip, the Luxor recreates the era when Pharaohs ruled the Nile. If Cleopatra was alive today, we believe she would travel the Strip in style with this 1966 Cadillac DeVille Convertible Coupe as her royal barge. The famous Cadillac fins of the 50s were reined in from their outrageous heights under design chief Harley Earl, who retired in 1958. Earl's successor, Bill Mitchell, steered Cadillac into tighter styling that featured less chrome and a more chiseled appearance. This streamlined austerity found popular acclaim as America became obsessed with the space race and the clean lines of space-age design. At 0–60 MPH in 10 seconds and with near-silent performance at a top speed of 140 MPH, this Caddy beats a camel any day!

Below: You can get pretty hot in Las Vegas behind the wheel of a fast-moving betty like this 1968 Shelby GT500 KR (that's for King of the Road). Designer Carroll Shelby's convertible is actually a fish-out-of-water in Vegas: it's one of only 318 built with the California surfboard option. This option featured a surfboard tie-down mounted on the roll bar, and, in keeping with the car's attention to detail, an actual surfboard color-coordinated with the car and trademark Shelby racing stripe. Nestled in pink stucco since its construction in 1956, the novelty portholes in the pool of the Glass Pool Inn accentuate the luxury of cooling off via an aquatic plunge in the parched desert heat.

Opposite: Have you met that special someone? Are you yearning to be united forever? Want to avoid unnecessary family drama? In short, are you ready to tie that knot right now? If so, we suggest a trip to Las Vegas's hub of happy matrimony—the Chapel of the Bells. This mint-condition Chevrolet Camaro Z28 Rally Sport might be destined more for the Fun City Motel at left. This is a classic muscle car that's designed for the seduction of speed. Chevrolet weighed in with the Camaro two years after Ford originated the Mustang and it was an instant hit. The Camaro's impressive power provided weekend racers lucky enough to own one with many a speedy thrill.

The corrugated metal roof of this carnival ride is a perfect foil for the aerodynamic edge of this 1966 Chevrolet Corvette 427 Convertible. The Corvette's gills accentuate that sharklike feeling: this baby is hungry for chum.

Perhaps the world's fastest looking car, this limited production 1969 Dodge Charger Daytona Hemi sports an enormous wing.

There may be no more flagrant a speed-demon car ever built than this 1970 Plymouth Superbird. Arriving at the end of Detroit's fuel-squandering era, the Superbird is a street-legal race car that was mass-produced only to meet NASCAR requirements for a production vehicle. Less than 2,000 Superbirds were made and only a few were sold to us mere mortals on the streets. Like an architectural version of the Superbird's spoiler are the wild golden arches of this McDonald's Restaurant in Downey, California. One of the few original surviving examples of the burger franchise that would come to dominate the world, this McDonald's has remained intact since 1953. It's a reminder of the days when the golden arches played a structural role as roof supports guaranteed to catch the eyes and appetites of passing motorists.

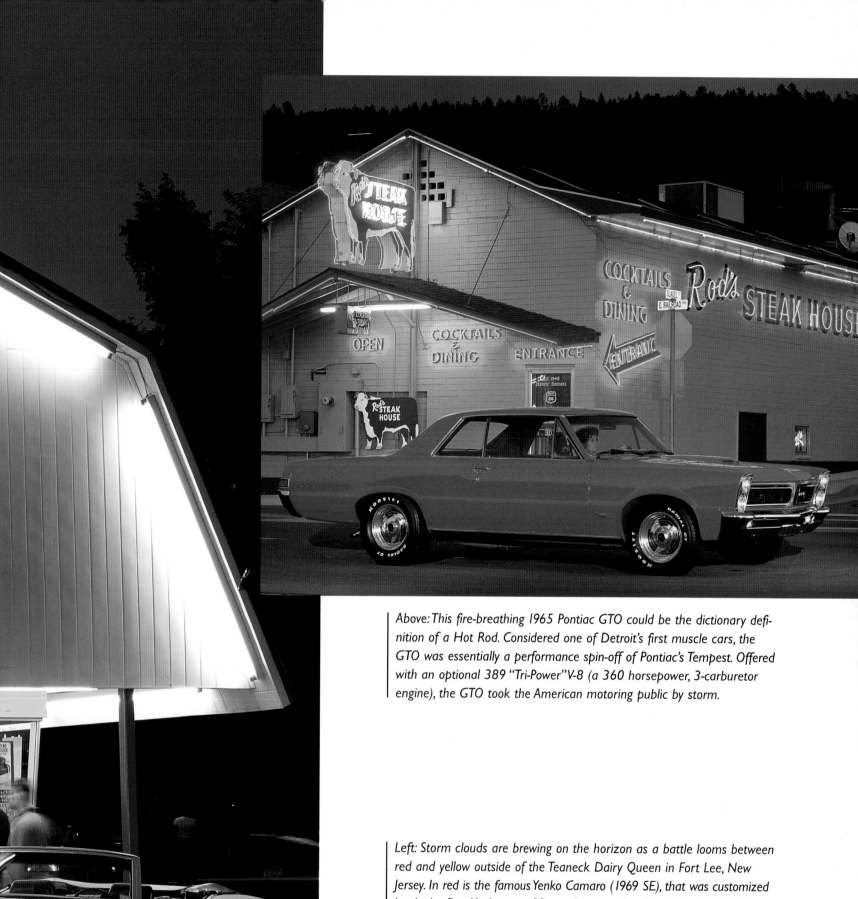

Above: This fire-breathing 1965 Pontiac GTO could be the dictionary definition of a Hot Rod. Considered one of Detroit's first muscle cars, the
GTO was essentially a performance spin-off of Pontiac's Tempest. Offered
with an optional 389 "Tri-Power" V-8 (a 360 horsepower, 3-carburetor
engine), the GTO took the American motoring public by storm.

Left: Storm clouds are brewing on the horizon as a battle looms between
red and yellow outside of the Teaneck Dairy Queen in Fort Lee, New
Jersey. In red is the famous Yenko Camaro (1969 SE), that was customized
by dealer Don Yenko out of Pennsylvania with a big-block 427 cid V-8:
these engines proved so popular that Chevy began supplying Yenko with
the engines pre-installed. Packing its own sting is this bumblebee yellow
Camaro, the quiet middle sibling between big Impala and little Nova. It's
secret weapon? The SS (Super-Sport) package that includes a 350+
horsepower V-8. When these babies get going that red roof better be
securely bolted to its vanilla moorings!

7.
DECLINE
AND
RESURRECTION
1971-1999

In the wake of the 1980s, some American automotive design has returned to a 1950s design vocabulary, spun with a uniquely 90s sense of irony. In his 1992 Chezoom Streetrod, hot rod builder Boyd Coddington signaled the way forward with rear fins that pay affectionate homage to the 1957 Chevy Bel Air, yet with a playful, larger-than-life feeling that might be termed "post-modern."

FOR A BRIEF TIME, LIFE IN AMERICA WAS A MOTORIST'S DREAM. There was plenty of room on those new four-lane roads and plenty of horsepower to tear them up. Life in the fast lane was hunky-dory. We loved our new ultra-efficient freeways—bypassing the small towns sure saved time: even if we missed the home cookin' of our favorite mom-and-pop restaurants.

Detroit's muscle cars became so fast nothing could stop them. You could drive one straight off the showroom floor onto the race-track. Nothing stopped those fuel-breathing monsters until they ran into the crippling hurdle of the 1973 Arab oil embargo. Suddenly there were long gas lines. Drivers traded tales of woe as spiraling gas prices became a national obsession. The unprecedented concept of carpools

This 1996 Plymouth Prowler goes straight back to the joy of souped-up hot rods and street racing in the 1950s. An unambiguous fun-car with sophisticated technology, the Prowler attracts attention wherever it goes. This is the car for boomers who didn't get enough American Graffiti the first time around, but it's also perfectly suited to Silicon Valley's post-adolescent moguls after their first IPO.

for adults arose when people couldn't get enough gas to drive in the usual one-man/family-per-vehicle ratio.

Washington, D.C., had a solution—"55 Saves Lives." A nation addicted to driving suddenly was confined to the "maximum fuel efficiency speed" of 55 MPH. Overnight, the new lower speed limits hypnotized drivers into wondering what hit them. We willingly traded our two-lane America for the high speed and safety of the interstates, but at 55 MPH the interstates were a real snooze. We began to miss our classic American roadside strips and lament the boredom of the highway.

The Highway Beautification Act of 1972 limited the number and size of highway signs. As roadside consumers we only had the generic "approved" signs along the freeway indicating gas, food, and lodging from which to make our choice. No chance to case the joint before we pulled off the interstate. No wonder there was such a rise in the number of franchised businesses. Gone were the eccentric ad campaigns that allowed us to ponder whether to patronize an independently owned motel or restaurant: now we had to make our roadside decisions in seconds, based on corporate logos alone:

"It seemed so much more interesting to travel on those routes and stay in the small motels along the way, and stop at those old country restaurants than it does now on all those interstate highways. In those days, you would drive through all those small towns. And now you don't even know you go by them except to exit. You may get there a little quicker, but you don't get to see the real America as we did back then. Yes, things were simpler and slower then."

—Ed Rexius, Saginaw, Michigan

Suddenly discovering ourselves in a fuel-efficient era, Americans abandoned Detroit's fuel-slurping monsters and gravitated to what we could afford—Japanese econo-boxes. Detroit was a deer in the headlights of the cars flowing in from Japan. Higher gasoline prices had been the rule in the rest of the world; foreign auto manufacturers had long ago adapted their cars accordingly. For the first time, Detroit had to play catch-up in a brand new game it took them years to understand. Unable to win the efficiency race with horsepower or chrome, Detroit took years to engineer their way out of trouble.

The oil embargo changed the roadside as well. Self-serve gasoline pumps, an innovation pio-

Below: The mechanistic design of this 1987 Lamborghini Countach is reminiscent of the evil Death Star, bastion of power for Darth Vader in the hit movie Star Wars.

neered in California, boomed as customers opted to "pump their own" and save a buck or two. It didn't take long for gas station operators to figure out that as long as we were already out of our cars to serve as our own grease jockeys, we might buy a soda, or a quart of milk, or a cheese dog, or an air freshener in the shape of a tree.

Convenience stores like 7-Eleven boomed and the gas 'n gro was brought back from the cast-off bin. Remember early motoring days when the gas pump was on the curb outside of the general store? Well, it's still a gas 'n gro world except today's grocery is second fiddle to the numerous pumps that line our highways.

At the close of the twentieth century, falling gas prices, ended years of paranoia left over from the energy crisis. In that giddy era, we fell back into an age of automotive exuberance. Today, the 1950s infatuation with "bigger is better" rules again, only now we've replaced the 50s craze for tail fins with Sport Utility Vehicles—two-ton or more behemoths that swill fuel like hogs at the trough.

SUV's are today's fastest growing automotive segment. Their enormous size only adds to the delays on our over-burdened highway system. Traffic is nearing the standstill of two-lane America in the 1920s. One

Below: 1998 Porsche 959S detail

Opposite: One of the most coveted Porsches in recent memory, the 1988 Porsche 959 was barred from import into the U.S. by the Environmental Protection Agency. A loophole allowed for the importation of a few examples designed specifically for racetrack use. Hence this 959S (for sport) is one of the rarest Porsche models of recent years and a true object of 1980s desire.

can almost understand the impulse toward Detroit's monster SUV's as sheer protection against the number of vehicles on the road.

Today in Los Angeles (where the car is king) it's entirely possible to spend an entire day without leaving the car. The dedicated Angeleno will leave the house in the morning with a cooler containing special treats not available at the drive-thru restaurants he will patronize. Errands to run? No problem—drive-thru cleaners and convenience stores have adapted themselves to our car-crazed world. E-mail and faxes enter the car through the cigarette lighter while we yak on our cellular phones in five lanes of bumper-to-bumper traffic.

No longer is this congestion limited to L.A., its famous capital. Major metropolitan areas throughout the country are contending with record levels of traffic, as one-time suburbs are becoming urban centers in a never-ending sprawl.

After a hundred years of the automobile, once again we find ourselves in an age of automotive exuberance. The hard-won frugality of the 1970s and 80s has been tossed aside as we thrilled to the

1990s joys of cheap gas and oversized cars. But with this automotive dream comes the reality of automotive excess: problems with traffic, safety, and overconsumption of resources threatens to overtake us. At the dawn of the twenty-first century, a newly reinvigorated OPEC has once again made gas prices an issue. Will the price per gallon bring the SUV dinosaurs to their knees?

No matter what the future brings, the transcendental quality of the highway still remains if you're willing to take the road less traveled.

"This was once a major road between Los Angeles and Chicago, and I can't imagine the goods of commerce passing this way. How time has changed the events of the past decades, and yet what is truly important has stayed the same. The quiet isolation, the clean, clear sky at night that revealed every constellation, the faces of the native Americans, which told a story without speaking a word."

—Gerard Smith, Tallahassee, Florida

Opposite: More than any other SUV, the Grand Cherokee is responsible for stoking the sports utility craze of the 1990s. Originally designed as an off-road vehicle, the Grand Cherokee has become the preferred conveyance of soccer moms, virtual dads, and other suburban and semi-urban family configurations.

Right: This 1993 Jeep Wrangler resembles the original military vehicle in World War II. Perhaps because its utilitarian lines look ever ready for off-road activity, the Wrangler has become a coveted urban symbol in the "anything can happen" 1990s.

Above: Young moguls have to start somewhere, and this 1993 Honda Civic Coupe offered higher quality and reliability at a lower price than most Detroit cars could muster at the time. With their low profile and surprising performance, many economy cars allow their drivers to enjoy pushing the speed limit, unlike the flashier sports-car drivers, who tend to elicit the wrath of the police.

Left: As with sports cars and showboat vehicles, the pickup truck is another 1950s automotive genre that scored a powerful comeback in the 1990s. Some things never change, and the American desire to haul cargo is one of them. The Johnny Rockets chain of classic diners in Los Angeles also stays true to its heritage, offering an unaltered 50s tradition of burgers, dogs, and fries around the clock.

The object of many an adolescent (and post-adolescent) fantasy is this 1991 Lamborghini Diablo. The super-low-slung Lamborghini has a few things in common with visiting a shrink: it's expensive and you lie back so flat (on the richest leather seating) that your deepest feelings are bound to well up when you take off down the road. It's a bargain compared to yacht racing, which George Plimpton once described as "standing in a cold shower tearing up hundred dollar bills."

Like a desert wind, this silver Porsche 1989 911 S has speed, grace, and mystery. The double-bubble over the convertible roof gives the car the smooth lines of a mirage.

The Golden Gate looms high above this rare, low-slung 1980 BMW M1. Created at a time of corporate soul searching, the M1 was BMW's bold attempt to create a sports car that could run nose-to-nose with the Ferrari. Needless to say, they succeeded.

Below: The deeply streaked flanks of this 1986 Ferrari Testarossa look like they could stabilize a jet. Featuring consummate Ferrari engineering, the Testarossa was dressed up in a flashy skin that epitomized the 1980s era of conspicuous consumption described by Tom Wolfe in Bonfire of the Vanities. Tricked out in Nancy Reagan red, this Ferrari commands total attention wherever it goes, tempting some to call it the "Testosterossa."

Above: With dual intercoolers and a dual turbo, the engine of this 1985 Ferrari GTO exemplifies 80s ambition. One could imagine Gordon Gecko from the movie Wall Street revving the 12 cylinders beneath this hood.

Right: The ultimate status symbol for flourishing American capitalists, the 1990 F40.

This 1992 Lexus SC-400 is emblematic of the inroads Japan made on the luxury car market in the 1990s. After flooding the American market with economy cars in the late 1970s and 1980s, the Japanese bested the Germans in the luxury car market via the Lexus. The key advantage of the Lexus was its incredible reliability, which the more persnickety German cars had never quite been able to pull off despite high levels of luxury and craftsmanship.

Here's a car from the go-go 1980s—a two-door Pontiac Grand Prix in the neon red-light district of the Sunset Strip. Note the opera window—a vintage styling motif that has passed out of favor in recent years. That, along with the rakish curve of the hood, recalls 1970s styling. This particular model happens to be a favorite of the "low rider" crowd, and can be seen in modified form cruising the streets of Hollywood.

Above: Looking like a vehicle from Neptune, this Pontiac Protosport concept car features a host of stylistic innovations from the past and future. The gull-wing doors and tungsten headlights make this car truly a post-space-age vehicle. It's a design approach that opens a whole new world of possibilities.

Left: Chrysler was an endangered company on the edge of dissolution in the late 1980s. This 1992 Dodge Viper RT/10 represents their bold attempt to stage the return of the classic American sports car as well as to bolster their chances of corporate survival. The gambit paid off: the Viper became a sensational showpiece that drew the public back to Chrysler showrooms. Hence the Viper's sting spurred Chrysler's recovery.

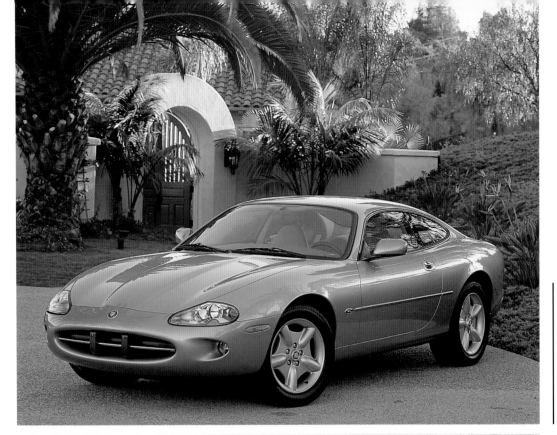

The 1997 XK8 is Jaguar's first all-new model since the XJS of the early 1970s. Jaguar faithful were alarmed that Ford's corporate takeover would mean the end of this marquee's unique character. Fortunately, Ford added a needed boost of reliability, but preserved the classic Jaguar aura.

The E-series represents Mercedes's attempt to update their superb, but rather stolid cars into a more youthful mode. This 1999 Mercedes Benz E430 features lighter, more expressive styling than its predecessors. After all, the older generation still has the classic S-class to fall back on.

The 1998 Cadillac Evoq concept is a turn of the millennium stylistic manifesto for Cadillac. With brave new styling and technological innovations like night vision (aerospace technology that projects an image of the road onto the windshield in dark driving conditions), the Evoq signals Cadillac's determination to define the direction of cars in the 21st century. Cadillac's operating philosophy is "art and science"—cutting-edge research endowing American luxury cars with unparalleled technological refinement.

Rather like Andy Warhol's famous soup can, the 1998 New Beetle is Volkswagen's audacious pop-art interpretation of the old Beetle. But the mechanics are strictly state-of-the-art, with running gear borrowed from the popular Golf, and handling to match.

Saturday night,
Myrtle Beach,
South Carolina

Best bellies, Los Angeles

A & W Rootbeer, Visalia, California

Tourist trap, New Mexico

Above: Foot-long hot dog, Myrtle Beach, South Carolina
Opposite: Bulldozer preacher, North Carolina

Volkswagen Beetle, Yucatan, Mexico

Dinosaur, Cabazon, California

Above: Desert hot rod, Kingman, Arizona
Right: Mojave desert, Arizona

Above: Twin Arrows, Arizona
Opposite: Spaceman, Wilmington, Illinois

Stuckey's, New Mexico

Above: Shakes, St. Louis, Missouri

Opposite: Ablaze from the lights of the arid night heat, this sumptuous 1965 Chevrolet Corvette Roadster is a powerful customer ready for some real partying in the kind of neighborhood where they don't ask why. The 1963–67 Corvettes are considered by many arbiters to be unrivalled in terms of design and performance. Chief designer Bill Mitchell refined the Corvette's knife's-edge body with extensive wind-tunnel testing while head engineer Zora Arkus-Duntov ensured that the mechanics underlying the hood were every bit as powerful as the exterior was suave. When this Corvette entered Albuquerque, Route 66 became Central Avenue, a thoroughfare where Jack's Liquor Store and other establishments are ready and waiting to provide a good time for all.

INDEX OF CARS

EDITOR: Ruth A. Peltason

DESIGNER: Dana Sloan

Library of Congress Cataloging-in-Publication Data

Lewis, Lucinda.
    Roadside America: the automobile and the American dream / Lucinda Lewis.
        p. cm.
    ISBN 0–8109–4434–0
        1. Automobiles—United States. 2. Automobiles—Social aspects—
    United States. 3. Popular culture—United States. I. Title

TL23 .L424 2000
303.48'32–dc21   00–21034

Copyright © 2000 Lucinda Lewis / Machine Age

Published in 2000 by Harry N. Abrams, Incorporated, New York
All rights reserved. No part of the contents of this book may be reproduced
without the written permission of the publisher

Printed and bound in Hong Kong

 Harry N. Abrams, Inc.
100 Fifth Avenue
New York, N.Y. 10011
www.abramsbooks.com

St. Louis Community College
at Meramec
Library